Praise for *The Fire This Time*

"*The Fire This Time* is a powerful, rewarding read that gets to the heart of what it means to be black in America today."

—*The Root*

"A stirring anthology that takes more cues from Baldwin than just its title . . . Every poem and essay in Ward's volume remains grounded in a harsh reality that our nation, at large, refuses fully to confront."

—*The New York Times Book Review*

"Ward's remarkable achievement is the gift of freshly minted perspectives on a tale that may seem old and twice-told. Readers in search of conversations about race in America should start here."

—*Publishers Weekly* (starred review)

"With this gorgeous chorus Ward has . . . created a world, a space, the one she, herself, was seeking. A new type of belonging, a new place to belong, is exactly what she has given us."

—*The Los Angeles Review of Books*

"To Baldwin's call we now have a choral response—one that should be read by every one of us committed to the cause of equality and freedom."

—Jelani Cobb, historian

"This is a book that seeks to place the shock of our own times into historical context and, most importantly, to move these times forward."

—*Vogue*

"The writing is impressive: literary, insightful, urgent, timely, a bracing antiseptic to still-open racial wounds. . . . Fifty-three years, two civil rights movements, and one black president after Baldwin's original, the problem with a book like this is that we still need a book like this."

—*Minneapolis Star Tribune*

"A powerful book . . . alive with purpose, conviction, and intellect."

—*The New York Times*

"The prose and poetry contained in this concise volume, written by literary luminaries such as Pulitzer Prize winner Isabel Wilkerson and National Book Critics Circle Award recipient Edwidge Danticat, is illuminating and even cathartic. . . . Ward's reflections on race and racism, along with those of seventeen other writers, are thoughtful, searing, and at times, hopeful."

—*USA Today*

"The generation of segregation gave us *The Fire Next Time*. . . . We broke down those walls. . . . The generation after segregation gives us the water to mix with the ashes to build . . . something . . . anything all . . . in the words of Margaret Walker . . . our own. This is a book to pick up and tuck under our hearts to see what we can build."

—Nikki Giovanni, poet

"[*The Fire This Time*] reveals the burdens of history, memory, and identity in these troubling times. . . . Ward has curated a book, with some of the best contemporary writers of color in the country, to help us feel and think our way through this current moment."

—*Time*

"In *The Fire This Time*, National Book Award winner Jesmyn Ward has gathered a stunning roster of contemporary writers of color to reflect on race in the present, and in the shadow of the past. . . . [It is] both timely and potentially timeless. Its subjects, blackness and black people, are at the root of the US nation-state, the ever-present other, still so often the source of its poetry, pain, and promise, and here in this book they, too, sing America."

—*San Francisco Chronicle*

"A powerful reminder that meaningful discussions about Black lives mattering must 'acknowledge the plantation, must unfold white sheets, and the black diaspora.' . . . African-American intellectuals and activists are finding a collective voice."

—*Florida Courier*

"An absolutely indispensable anthology."

—*Booklist* (starred review)

"One of the necessary books of our time."

—The Buffalo News

"Black brilliance continues to fight an uphill battle. Its luminosity inevitably collides with the stubborn desire of many Americans to place the white experience smack-dab in the middle of the story, an inclination tantamount to hiding our light under a bushel. . . . [Ward] believes 'that sharing our stories confirms our humanity. That it creates community, both within our own community and beyond it.' She burns and she hopes. I hope too, for all our sakes, that she is right."

—Bookforum

"A powerful group of writers."

—Chicago Tribune

"*The Fire This Time* freely weds the political with the personal in unconventional and often lyrical ways. . . . In this probing twenty-first-century breakdown of what it means to be black, we're telling everything. It's about time."

—In These Times

"Vital to living in our times . . . An extraordinary anthology . . . Ward's book deepens and enlarges with each piece."

—The Boston Globe

"Timely contributions to an urgent national conversation."

—Kirkus Reviews

"What do we do, this post–civil rights generation, in the face of the same injustice, dressed in different clothes, coded in different laws? In *The Fire This Time*, a new generation of black writers speak with the 'fierce urgency of now.'"

—Ayana Mathis, novelist

"Groundbreaking."

—Library Journal

Also by Jesmyn Ward

Sing, Unburied, Sing: A Novel
Men We Reaped: A Memoir
Salvage the Bones: A Novel
Where the Line Bleeds: A Novel

THE FIRE
THIS TIME

A New Generation
Speaks about Race

EDITED BY

Jesmyn Ward

SCRIBNER

New York   London   Toronto   Sydney   New Delhi

SCRIBNER
An Imprint of Simon & Schuster, Inc.
1230 Avenue of the Americas
New York, NY 10020

First Scribner paperback edition June 2017

SCRIBNER and design are registered trademarks of The Gale Group, Inc.,
used under license by Simon & Schuster, Inc., the publisher of this work.

For information about special discounts for bulk purchases,
please contact Simon & Schuster Special Sales at 1-866-506-1949
or business@simonandschuster.com.

The Simon & Schuster Speakers Bureau can bring authors to your live event.
For more information or to book an event, contact the Simon & Schuster Speakers
Bureau at 1-866-248-3049 or visit our website at www.simonspeakers.com.

Interior design by Erich Hobbing

Manufactured in the United States of America

5   7   9   10   8   6

Library of Congress Control Number: 2016005371

ISBN 978-1-5011-2634-5
ISBN 978-1-5011-2635-2 (pbk)
ISBN 978-1-5011-2636-9 (ebook)

Copyright notices continued on page 225.

To Trayvon Martin
and the many other black men, women, and children
who have died and been denied justice
for these last four hundred years

Contents

CONTENTS

PART III: JUBILEE

THE FIRE THIS TIME

The Tradition

JERICHO BROWN

Aster. Nasturtium. Delphinium. We thought
Fingers in dirt meant it was our dirt, learning
Names in heat, in elements classical
Philosophers said could change us. *Star Gazer.*
Foxglove. Summer seemed to bloom against the will
Of the sun, which news reports claimed flamed hotter
On this planet than when our dead fathers
Wiped sweat from their necks. *Cosmos. Baby's Breath.*
Men like me and my brothers filmed what we
Planted for proof we existed before
Too late, sped the video to see blossoms
Brought in seconds, colors you expect in poems
Where the world ends, everything cut down.
John Crawford. Eric Garner. Mike Brown.

Introduction

JESMYN WARD

After George Zimmerman shot and killed Trayvon Martin on February 26, 2012, I took to Twitter. I didn't have anywhere else to go. I wanted to hear what others, black writers and activists, were thinking about what happened in Sanford, Florida. Twitter seemed like a great social forum, a virtual curia, a place designed to give us endless voice in declarations of 140 characters or fewer.

I found the community I sought there. I found so many people giving voice to my frustration, my anger, and my fear. We shared news and updates and photos, anything we could find about Trayvon. During that time, I was pregnant, and I was revising a memoir about five young black men I'd grown up with, who all died young, violent deaths. Every time I logged in or read another article about Trayvon, my unborn child and my dead brother and my friends sat with me. I imagined them all around me, our faces long with dread. Before Zimmerman was acquitted of second-degree murder and manslaughter in July 2013, I suspected Trayvon's death would be excused. During this period, I returned often to the photo of Trayvon wearing a pale hoodie. As I gazed on his face—his jaw a thin blade, his eyes dark and serious, too big in the way that children's eyes are—I saw a child. And it seemed that no one outside of Black Twitter was saying this: I read article after article that others shared on Twitter, and no major news outlet was stating the obvious. Trayvon Martin was a seventeen-year-old child, legally and biologically; George Zimmerman was an adult. An adult shot and killed a child while the child was walking home from a convenience store where he'd purchased Skittles and a cold drink. Everything, from Zimmerman stalking and shooting Trayvon to the way Trayvon was tried in the court of public opinion after his death, seemed insane. How could anyone look at Trayvon's baby face and not see a child? And not feel an innate desire to protect, to cherish? How?

And then I realized most Americans did not see Trayvon Martin as I did. Trayvon's sable skin and his wide nose and his tightly coiled hair signaled something quite different for others. Zimmerman and the jury and the media outlets who questioned his character with declarations like *He abused marijuana* and *He was disciplined at school for graffiti and possessing drug paraphernalia* saw Trayvon as nothing more than a wayward thug. They didn't see him as an adult human being, either, but as some kind of ravenous hoodlum, perpetually at the mercy of his animalistic instincts. Although this was never stated explicitly, his marijuana use and adolescent mischief earned this hoodlum in a hoodie his death.

I knew that myth. It was as familiar to me as my own eyes, my own nose, my own hair, my own fragile chest. It was as familiar to me as the air I grew up in, air as dense and heavy and close and hot as the air Trayvon breathed before Zimmerman shot him. I, too, grew up in a place that could sometimes feel as limiting and final as being locked in an airtight closet, the air humid and rank with one's own breath and panic. A place where for all the brilliant, sun-drenched summer days, there is sometimes only the absence of light: America, and the American South. A place where the old myths still hold a special place in many white hearts: the rebel flag, Confederate monuments, lovingly restored plantations, *Gone with the Wind*. A place where black people were bred and understood to be animals, a place where some feel that the Fourteenth Amendment and *Brown v. Board of Education* are only the more recent in a series of unfortunate events. A place where black life has been systematically devalued for hundreds of years.

In December 2002, my then senator, Trent Lott, attended a function honoring the outgoing Senator Strom Thurmond, who is famous for opposing the Civil Rights Act of 1957 so strenuously he conducted the longest lone filibuster ever, one that lasted twenty-four hours and eighteen minutes. At this event, Lott, who is from a small town on the Mississippi Gulf Coast around twenty-five miles from mine, said: "We're proud of it [voting for Thurmond in the 1948 presidential election]. And if the rest of the country had followed our lead, we wouldn't have had all these problems over all these years, either." It was dismaying to hear this, to see what those in power thought of people like me, but it wasn't a surprise. After all, when I participated in Presidential Classroom in Washington, D.C., I, along with around five of my high school classmates, met Senator Trent Lott.

My schoolmates were white. I was not. Trent Lott took a whip as long as a car off his office table, where it lay coiled and shiny brown, and said to my one male schoolmate who grinned at Lott enthusiastically: *Let's show 'em how us good old boys do it.* And then he swung that whip through the air and cracked it above our heads, again and again. I remember the experience in my bones.

I know little. But I know what a good portion of Americans think of my worth. Their disdain takes form. In my head, it is my dark twin. Sometimes I wonder which of us will be remembered if I die soon, if I suffocate in that closet. Will I be a vicious menace, like Trayvon Martin? An unhinged menace, like Tamir Rice? A monstrous menace, like Mike Brown? An unreasonable menace, like Sandra Bland? A sly menace, like Emmett Till? I imagine I will be as black and fetid as the horde at Scarlett's heels, crowding her wagon, thundering to rip it apart, wheel by rivet.

Replace ropes with bullets. Hound dogs with German shepherds. A gray uniform with a bulletproof vest. Nothing is new.

I needed words. The ephemera of Twitter, the way the voices of the outraged public rose and sank so quickly, flitting from topic to topic, disappointed me. I wanted to hold these words to my chest, take comfort in the fact that others were angry, others were agitating for justice, others could not get Trayvon's baby face out of their heads. But I could not. The nature of the application, even the nature of the quality journalism of the time, with so much of it published online, meant that I couldn't go to one place for it all. I couldn't fully satisfy my need for kinship in this struggle, commiserate with others trying to find a way out of that dark closet. In desperation, I sought James Baldwin.

I read Baldwin's essay "Notes of a Native Son" while I was in my mid-twenties, and it was a revelation. I'd never read creative nonfiction like Baldwin's, never encountered this kind of work, work that seemed to see me, to know I needed it. I read it voraciously, desperate for the words on the page. I needed to know that someone else saw the myriad injustices of living while black in this country, that someone so sharp and gifted and human could acknowledge it all, and speak on it again and again. Baldwin was so brutally honest. His prose was frank and elegant in turn, and I returned to him annually after that first impression-forming read. Around a year after Trayvon Martin's death, a year in which black person after black person died and no one was held accountable, I picked up *The Fire Next Time*, and I read: "You can only be destroyed by believing that you really are what the white world calls a *nigger*. I tell you this because I love you, and please don't you ever forget it." It was as if I sat on my porch steps with a wise father, a kind, present uncle, who said this to me. Told me I was worthy of love. Told me I was worth something in the world. Told me I was a human being. I saw Trayvon's face, and all the words blurred on the page.

It was then that I knew I wanted to call on some of the great thinkers and extraordinary voices of my generation to help me puzzle this out. I knew that a black boy who lives in the hilly deserts of California, who likes to get high with his friends on the weekend and who freezes in a prickly sweat whenever he sees blue lights in his rearview, would need a book like this. A book that would reckon with the fire of rage and despair and fierce, protective love currently sweeping through the streets and campuses of America. A book that would gather new voices in one place, in a lasting, physical form, and provide a forum for those writers to dissent, to call to account, to witness, to reckon. A book that a girl in rural Missouri could pick up at her local library and, while reading, encounter a voice that hushed her fears. In the pages she would find a wise aunt, a more present mother, who saw her terror and despair threading their fingers through her hair, and would comfort her. We want to tell her this: *You matter. I love you. Please don't forget it.*

The Fire Next Time is roughly divided into two parts: a letter to Baldwin's nephew, which looks forward to the future, and an essay about religion and the Nation of Islam, which concerns itself with Baldwin's past and present. I initially thought that *The Fire This Time* would be divided into three parts, roughly inspired by Baldwin's chronological division: essays or poems about the past, deemed legacy, essays or poems about the present, labeled reckoning, and essays or poems about the future, or jubilee, and all of them would wrestle with the specters of race and history in America, and how those specters are haunting us now. But as the pieces of work my editor and I solicited came in, I realized that the structure I envisioned for the work would not be as tidy as I thought. But race in the United States is not a tidy matter. Only three of the submitted pieces explicitly referenced the future. Most of them were concerned with the past and the present. And that told me two things. First, it confirmed how inextricably interwoven the past is in the present, how heavily that past bears on the future; we cannot talk about black lives mattering or police brutality without reckoning with the very foundation of this country. We must acknowledge the plantation, must unfold white sheets, must recall the black diaspora to understand what is happening now. Second, it reveals a certain exhaustion, I think. We're tired. We're tired of having to figure out how to talk to our kids and teach them that America sees them as less, and that she just might kill them. This is the conversation we want to avoid. We're tired of feeling futile in the face of this ever-present danger, this omnipotent history, predicated as this country is, founded as this country was, on our subjugation. But the pieces in this work that do invoke the future—Daniel José Older's letter to his wife and future child, Natasha Trethewey's poem about the many planes on which time exists, and Edwidge Danticat's essay exploring the idea that people of the black diaspora are refugees—help me to believe that I might be able to have that conversation with my child in the future. These pieces give me words that I might use to push past the fear and exhaustion and speak to my daughter, my nieces and nephews. This work helps me to believe that this is worthwhile work, and that our troubling the water is worthy.

If I were smarter, perhaps I wouldn't say this, but I attest to this because I feel it: all these essays give me hope. I believe there is power in words, power in asserting our existence, our experience, our lives, through words. That sharing our stories confirms our humanity. That it creates community, both within our own community and beyond it. Maybe someone who didn't perceive us as human will think differently after reading Garnette Cadogan's essay on the black body in space, or after reading Emily Raboteau's work on urban murals. Perhaps after reading Kiese Laymon's essay on black artists and black love and OutKast, or after reading Mitchell S. Jackson's piece on composite fathers, a reader might see those like me anew. Maybe after reading Rachel Kaadzi Ghansah's essay on Baldwin or Kevin Young's hilarious essay about Rachel Dolezal and what it means to be black, a reader might cry in sympathy and then rise to laughter, and in doing so, feel kinship.

At the end of *The Fire Next Time*, Baldwin writes:

This past, the Negro's past, of rope, fire, torture, castration, infanticide, rape; death and humiliation; fear by day and night, fear as deep as the marrow of the bone; doubt that he was worthy of life, since everyone around him denied it; sorrow for his women, for his kinfolk, his children, who needed his protection, and whom he could not protect; rage, hatred, and murder, hatred for white men so deep that it often turned against him and his own, and made all love, all trust, all joy impossible—this past, this endless struggle to achieve and reveal and confirm a human identity, human authority, yet contains, for all its horror, something very beautiful . . . people who cannot suffer can never grow up, can never discover who they are. . . . Everything now, we must assume, is in our hands; we have no right to assume otherwise. If we—and now I mean the relatively conscious whites and the relatively conscious blacks, who must, like lovers, insist on, or create, the consciousness of others—do not falter in our duty now, we may be able, handful that we are, to end the racial nightmare, and achieve our country, and change the history of the world. If we do not dare everything, the fulfillment of that prophecy, re-created from the Bible in song by the slave, is upon us: *God gave Noah the rainbow sign, No more water, the fire next time!*

I hope this book makes each one of you, dear readers, feel as if we are sitting together, you and me and Baldwin and Trethewey and Wilkerson and Jeffers and Walters and Anderson and Smith and all the serious, clear-sighted writers here—and that we are composing our story together. That we are writing an epic wherein black lives carry worth, wherein black boys can walk to the store and buy candy without thinking they will die, wherein black girls can have a bad day and be mouthy without being physically assaulted by a police officer, wherein cops see twelve-year-old black boys playing with fake guns as silly kids and not homicidal maniacs, wherein black women can stop to ask for directions without being shot in the face by paranoid white homeowners.

I burn, and I hope.

PART I

LEGACY

Homegoing, AD

KIMA JONES

Here's the down south story we didn't tell you: sixteen hours in and Jack can't feel her feet but we never stop. Our uncle asleep at the wheel and we that closer to death with each mile. Turned around again and again, before GPS, we learned North Carolina is a long state: tobacco taller than us, the fields and fields of it, no washing it out of our clothes, the air so wet and thick of it, choking us.

Jack won't fly. Full grown with a dead granddaddy and still she won't fly, she tells us I-95 has always been the way back home so we gun it. Straight through, no stopping, sixteen hours and Jack doesn't care how bad we need to pee, she says, *Hold it.* Sixteen hours till we saw the palmetto trees and smelled the paper mill and knew Savage Road was in sight.

Georgie 'n' em got Grandaddy laid out in the front room like a piece of furniture and ushers fanning the top of Grandmama's head. We couldn't find our place in the business of departing: hams out the oven, lemon cake iced, organ tuned, tea made, napkins folded, the children's black patent leather shoes set out for the dirt road come morning.

Here's the down south story we didn't tell you: Leroy barking at us from the grill because when did everybody stop eating pork and why he got separate meat and when all the women become Nefertiti bangles and headwraps and all us named like Muslims. Our cousins who couldn't make it because he died on the wrong Friday, wadn't payday, and our cousins who did and their many children tearing up the front yard. Our decision to sneak into the woods with red cups, black and milds, Jim Beam, a blue lighter plucked from the card table, and Toya's gold cap kept in her change purse. The pot of greens we brought out with us and the mosquitoes keeping company like we wasn't down in the swamps to bury our dead.

Our cousins know the dark and the heat, but we haven't been home in so long. Our back sweating and this old bra sticky so more and more from the red cup. Our cousin say, *Lemme top it off for youse,* so we oblige and when he said pull, we pulled and when he said blow, we blew smoke over our shoulder and then into his open mouth, giggling. Our cousin say, *You know they found him in the bed, right?* And we nod cuz sleep don't come easy no how. He say, *Just like that.* And our cousin clap when he say *that* and we think of Grandaddy setting his glasses down on the nightstand one last time. Our cousin say, *You missed me?* And we smile cuz his hand is on our hip and it's hot out and he smell good and it's the darkest Charleston has ever been. The dead of night is forgiving when you're kin. Grandaddy gone and we sitting up in the woods with brown liquor, necking, our cousin hard on our thigh. Toya say, *Keep watch for them copperheads,* but copperheads ain't never kill nobody—we got our eyes trained for gators.

16

We think we can still outrun 'em.

Who threw that rock at the gator?
                              Don't know   *Where Toya?*

Y'all there?

                                   We here.

                    Gator comin, boy, run

  Don't see no gator, cuh   *Well, gator see us, nigga*

Runnnnnnnnnnnnnnnnnnnnnnnnnnnnnnnnnnnnnnnnnnnnnnnnnnnnnn
nnnnnnnnnnnnnnnnnnn

      so we run

                    fast

cuz gator made for water   but children born for land.

The Weight

RACHEL KAADZI GHANSAH

It was an acquaintance's idea to go there, to Baldwin's house. He knew from living in Paris that Baldwin's old place, the house where Baldwin died, was near an elegant and renowned hotel in the Côte d'Azur region of France. He said that both places were situated in a medieval-era walled town that was scenic enough to warrant the visit. He said we could go to Jimmy's house and then walk up the road for drinks at the hotel bar where Baldwin used to drink in the evening. He said we would make a day of it, that I wouldn't regret it.

For the first time in my life I was earning a bit of money from my writing, and since I was in London anyway for family obligations I decided to take the train over to Nice to meet him. But I remained apprehensive. Having even a tiny bit of disposable cash was very new and bizarre to me. It had been years since I had I bought myself truly new clothes, years since going to a cash machine to check my balance hadn't warranted a sense of impending doom, and years since I hadn't on occasion regretted even going to college because it was increasingly evident that I would never be able to pay back my loans. There were many nights where

I lay awake turning over in my mind the inevitable, that soon Sallie Mae or some faceless, cruel moneylender with a blues-song-type name would take my mother's home—she had cosigned for me—and thus render my family homeless. In my mind, three generations of progress would be undone by my vain commitment to tell stories about black people in a country where the black narrative was a quixotic notion at best. If I knew anything about being black in America it was that nothing was guaranteed, you couldn't count on a thing, and all that was certain for most of us was a black death. In my mind, a black death was a slow death, the accumulation of insults, injuries, neglect, second-rate health care, high blood pressure and stress, no time for self-care, no time to sigh, and in the end, the inevitable, the erasing of memory. I wanted to write against this, and so I was writing a history of the people who I did not want to forget. For many years, I taught during the day and wrote at night—long pieces, six thousand words for which I was paid two hundred bucks. I loved it; nothing else mattered because I was remembering, I was staving off death.

So I was in London when a check with one comma hit my account. It wasn't much but to me it seemed enormous. I decided if I was going to spend any money, something I was reluctant, if not petrified, to do, at the very least I would feel best about spending it on James Baldwin. After all, my connection to him was an unspoken hoodoo-ish belief that he had been the high priest in charge of my prayer of being a black person who wanted to exist on books and words alone. It was a deification that was fostered years before during a publishing internship. Basically, during a lonely week I had spent in the storeroom of a magazine's editorial office organizing the archives from 1870 to 2005, I had once found time to pray intensely at the altar of Baldwin. I had asked him to grant me endurance and enough fight so that I could exit that storeroom with my confidence intact. I told him what all writers chant to keep on, that I had a story to tell. But later, away from all of that, I quietly felt repelled by him—as if he were a home I had to leave to become my own. Instead, I had spent years immersing myself in the books of Sergei Dovlatov, Vivian Gornick, Henry Dumas, Sei Shōnagon, John McPhee, and bell hooks. Baldwin didn't need my prayers, he had the praise of the entire world.

I still liked Baldwin but in a divested way, the way that anyone who writes and aspires to write well does. When people asked me my opinion on him I told them the truth: that Baldwin had set the stage for every American essayist who came after him. One didn't need to worship him, or desire to emulate him, to know this and respect him for it. And yet, for me, there had always been something slightly off-putting about him—the strangely accented, ponderous way he spoke in the interviews I watched; the lofty, precious way in which he appeared in an essay by Joan Didion as the bored, above-it-all figure that white people revered because he could stay collected while the streets boiled. What I resented about Baldwin wasn't even his fault. I didn't like how many men who only cared about Ali, Coltrane, and Obama praised him as the black authorial exception. I didn't like how every essay about race cited him. I didn't like that he and my grandfather were four years apart in age, but that Baldwin, as he was taught to me, had escaped to France and avoided his birth-righted fate whereas millions of black men his age had not. It seemed easy enough to fly in from France to protest, whereas it seemed straight hellish to live in it with no ticket out. It seemed to me that Baldwin had written himself into the world—and I wasn't sure what that meant in terms of his allegiances to our interiors as an everyday, unglamorous slog.

So even now I have no idea why I went. Why I took that high-speed train past the sheep farms, and the French countryside, past the brick villages and stone aqueducts until the green hills faded and grew into Marseille's tall, dusky pink apartments and the bucolic steppes gave way to blue water where yachts and topless women with leather for skin were parked.

It was on that train that I had time to consider the first time I started to revere Baldwin, something that had occurred ten years earlier, when I was accepted as an intern at one of the oldest magazines in the country. I had found out about the magazine only a few months before. A friend who let me borrow an issue made my introduction, but only after he spent almost twenty minutes questioning the quality of my high school education. How could I have never heard of such an influential magazine? I got rid of the friend and kept his copy. But still I had no idea of what to expect.

During my train ride into the city on my first day, I kept telling myself that I really had no reason to be nervous; after all, I had proven my capability not just once but twice.

Because the internship was unpaid I had to decline my initial acceptance to instead take a summer job and then reapply. When I arrived at the magazine's offices, the first thing I noticed was the stark futuristic whiteness. The entire place was a brilliant white except for the tight, gray carpeting.

The senior and associate editors' offices had sliding glass doors and the rest of the floor was divided into white-walled cubicles for the interns and the assistant editors. The windows in the office looked out over the city, and through the filmy morning haze I could see the cobalt blue of the Manhattan Bridge and the water tanks that spotted some of the city's roofs. The setting, the height, and the spectacular view were not lost on me. I had never before had any real business in a Manhattan skyscraper.

Each intern group consisted of four people; mine was made up of a recent Vassar grad, a hippie-ish food writer from California, and a dapper Princeton grad of Southeast Asian and Jewish descent. We spent the first part of the day learning our duties, which included finding statistics, assisting the editors with the magazine's features, fact-checking, and reading submissions. Throughout the day various editors stopped by and made introductions. Sometime after lunch the office manager came into our cubicle and told us she was cleaning out the communal fridge and we were welcome to grab whatever was in it. Eager to scavenge a free midday snack, we decided to take her up on the offer. As we walked down the hall the Princeton grad joked that because he and I were the only brown folks around we should be careful about taking any food because they might say we were looting. I had forgotten about the tragedy of that week, Hurricane Katrina, during the day's bustle, and somehow I had also allowed the fact that I am black to fade to the back of my thoughts, behind my stress and excitement. It was then that I was smacked with the realization that the walls weren't the only unusually white entities in the office—the editorial staff seemed to be strangely all white as well.

Because we were interns, neophytes, we spent the first week getting acquainted with each other and the inner workings of the magazine. Sometime toward the end of my first week, a chatty senior editor approached me in the corridor. During the course of our conversation I was informed that I was (almost certainly) the first black person to ever intern at the magazine and there had never been any black editors. I laughed it off awkwardly, only because I had no idea of what to say. I was too shocked. At the time of my internship the magazine was more than one hundred and fifty years old. It was a real *Guess Who's Coming to Dinner* moment. Except that I, being a child of the eighties, had never watched the film in its entirety, I just knew it starred Sidney Poitier, as a young, educated black man who goes to meet his white fiancée's parents. The film was set in the 1960s; I had been born in 1981.

When my conversation with the talkative editor ended I walked back to my desk and decided to just forget about it. Besides, I reasoned, it was very possible that the editor was just absentminded. I tried to forget it but I could not, and finally I casually asked another editor if it was true. He told me he thought there had been an Algerian-Italian girl many years ago, but he was not certain if she really "counted" as black. I was also alerted later to there being one editor who was half Filipina, half white. But when I asked how this dismal situation could be possible I was told that the lack of diversity was due to the lack of applications from people of color. As awkward as these comments were, they were made in the spirit of oblivious commonwealth. It was office chatter meant to make me feel like one of the gang, but instead of comforting my concerns they made me feel like an oddity.

On good days, being the first black intern meant having my work done quickly and sounding extra witty around the water cooler; it meant I was chipping away at the glass ceiling that seemed to top most of the literary world. But on bad days I gagged on my resentment and furiously wondered why I was selected. I became paranoid that I was merely a product of affirmative action, even though I knew I wasn't. I had completed the application not once but twice and never did I mention my race. Still, I never felt like I was actually good enough. And with my family and friends so proud of me, I felt like I could not burst their bubble with my insecurity and trepidation.

So when I was the only intern asked by the deputy editor to do physical labor and reorganize all of the old copies of the magazine in the freezing, dusty storeroom, I fretted in private. Was I asked because of my race or because that was merely one of my duties as the intern-at-large? There was no way to tell. I found myself most at ease with the other interns and the staff that did not work on the editorial side of the magazine, the security guards, the delivery guys, the office manager, and the folks at the front desk; among them the United Nations was almost represented. With them, I did not have to worry that one word pronounced wrong or one reference not known would reflect not just poorly on me but also on any black person who might apply after me.

I also didn't have to worry about that in that storeroom. There I could think. I realized three things spending a week in the back of that dismal storeroom. That yes, I was the only intern asked to do manual labor, but also that I was surrounded by two hundred years of the greatest American essays ever written, and I discovered that besides the physical archives and magazines stored there, the storeroom was also home to the old index card invoices that its writers used to file. In between my filing duties, I spent time searching those cards, and the one that was most precious to me was Baldwin's. In 1965, he was paid $350 for an essay that is now legend. The check went to his agent's office. There is nothing particularly spectacular about the faintly yellowed card except that its routineness suggested a kind of normalcy. It was human and it looped a great man back to the earth for me. And in that moment, Baldwin's eminence was a gift. Because he had made it out of the storeroom. He had taken a steamer away from being driven mad from maltreatment. His excellence had moved him beyond the realm of physical labor. He had disentangled himself from being treated like someone who was worthless or questioning his worth. And better yet, Baldwin was so good they wanted to preserve his memory. I would look at that card every day of that week.

Baldwin joined the pantheon of black people who were from that instructional generation of civil rights fighters.

On that train to Baldwin's house I thought more about this generation and about the seemingly vast divide between Baldwin and my grandfather. They had very little in common, except they were of the same generation, the same race, and were both fearless men, which in black America says a lot. Whereas Baldwin spent his life writing against a canon, writing himself into the canon, he was a black man who was recording the Homeric legend of his life himself; my grandfather simply wanted to live with dignity.

My grandfather liked to look on the bright side. Even when I visited him in Los Angeles for one of the last times, he insisted things weren't so bad. He was eking out a living on the money we sent and social security. My mother asked him to come east to stay with us, but he refused. He had lived in this building for almost fifty years, but now the upstairs neighbors were what he called "young bloods," guys who threatened to shoot him when he complained about their noise. The landlord wanted him out to raise the rent; he needed more money for the place. All my grandfather had were a few worn tracksuits and his rusted golf clubs. No one needed an eighty-year-old carpenter, no matter how clever he was: he'd worked hard but had made next to nothing. California had once been fertile ground for him, but in the end it, too, was bound to the country that had long seen him and us as subservient human beings. But my grandfather preferred not to focus on that sort of thing. What Baldwin understood is that to be black in America is to have the demand for dignity be at absolute odds with the national anthem.

From the outside, Baldwin's house looks ethereal. The saltwater air from the Mediterranean acts like a delicate scrim over the heat and the horizon, and the dry, craggy yard is wide and long and tall with cypress trees. I had prepared for the day by watching clips of him in his gardens. I read about the medieval frescos that had once lined the dining room. I imagined the dinners he had hosted for Josephine Baker and Beauford Delaney under a trellis of creeping vines and grape arbors. I imagined a house full of books and life.

I fell in love with Baldwin, because Baldwin didn't go to France because it was France. He was not full of naïve, empty admiration for Europe; as he once said in an interview: "If I were twenty-four now, I don't know if and where I would go. I don't know if I would go to France, I might go to Africa. You must remember when I was twenty-four there was really no Africa to go to, except Liberia. Now, though, a kid now . . . well, you see, something has happened which no one has really noticed, but it's very important: Europe is no longer a frame of reference, a standard-bearer, the classic model for literature and for civilization. It's not the measuring stick. There are other standards in the world."

Baldwin left the States for the primary reason that all emigrants do—because anywhere seems better than home. This freedom-seeking gay man, who deeply loved his sisters and brothers—biological and metaphorical—never left them at all. He preserved himself so he could stay alone. In France, I saw Baldwin didn't live the life of a wealthy man but he did live the life of a man who wanted to travel, to erect an estate that held a mood of his own design, where he could write as an outsider from the noise, alone in silence, with fearlessness.

Decades after his death in 1987, what I found left behind in Baldwin's house was something similar to what we experienced when I waded through my grandfather's effects after his house had burned down. Two months later, my grandfather would die from shock and stress caused by the fire. Baldwin's death, too, came at him hard and fast. In both houses, I found mail strewn on dirt piles in rooms that no longer had doors or windowpanes, entryways nailed over to prevent trespassers like us. In each case, clearly someone had forced entry in order to drink beer. The scattered, empty beer cans were recent additions, as were the construction postings from the company that was tasked with tearing the house down. So that nothing remained. No remembrance of the past. Not even the sense that a great man had once lived there.

James Baldwin lived in this house for more than twenty-five years, and all that was left were half a dozen pink teacups and turquoise saucers buried by the house's rear wall, orange trees that were heavy with fruit, but the fruit was bitter and sharp to the taste. We see Baldwin's name in connection to the present condition more often than we see Faulkner's, Whitman's, or Thoreau's. We can visit houses and places where they lived and imagine how their geography shaped the authors and our collective vocabulary. By next year, Baldwin's house will just be another private memory for those who knew it.

I do not know if I will ever see his house again. If I will be able to pull sour oranges from his trees and wonder if they were so bitter when he lived there. I do know that Baldwin died a black death.

For a while when I came back to the States, I started to send desperate e-mails to people who knew him that read:

> For the last two days, I've basically found myself frantically, maniacally looking for everything that I could find about Baldwin's life there. To be honest, I'm not at all sure what I am looking for, but when I walked up that steep little hill, past the orange and cypress trees out onto the main road, and looked back at his house, I just felt a compulsion to start asking people who knew him about his life in that house. The compound is almost gone, as they are in the process of demolishing it, and yet something about it and him seemed to still be very much there.

I sent those notes—feeling as hopeless as I sounded—because I wanted to save that building. Because I was scared that no one else would ever be able to see that Baldwin had a rainbow kitchen—an orange sink and purple shelves—in his guesthouse. I wanted someone else to wonder what he ate from this kitchen, who he loved, who stayed in this annex of his estate; did his love feel free in this kitchen, in this house where two men could embrace in private behind the ramparts of his home in another country? I wanted someone else to understand the private, black language found in one of Baldwin's last conversations with his brother David. Frail, sick, being carried to his deathbed in his brother's arms, what the world thought of him might as well have been an ocean away. In that moment, Baldwin didn't refer to French poets, or to the cathedrals of his genius, he instead returned to a popular Hollies song. He loved music, and he told his brother: So it is true what they say—he is my brother and he's not heavy.

Baldwin once wrote, "Life is tragic simply because the earth turns and the sun inexorably rises and sets, and one day, for each of us, the sun will go down for the last, last time. Perhaps the whole root of our trouble, the human trouble, is that we will sacrifice all the beauty of our lives, will imprison ourselves in totems, taboos, crosses, blood sacrifices, steeples, mosques, races, armies, flags, nations, in order to deny the fact of death, the only fact we have. It seems to me that one ought to rejoice in the fact of death— ought to decide, indeed, to earn one's death by confronting with passion the conundrum of life. One is responsible for life: It is the small beacon in that terrifying darkness from which we come and to which we shall return."

Because I am telling you this now, writing it all down, I am finding time to regard memory and death differently. I'm holding them up in the light and searching them, inspecting them, as they are not as I want them to be. On that hill, in Saint Paul de Vence, I wanted to alter fate, and preserve things. But why? They did not need me—Baldwin seemed to have prepared himself well for his black death, his mortality, and even better, his immortality. Indeed, he bested all of them, because he wrote it all down. And this is how his memory is carried. On the scent of wild lavender like the kind in his yard, in the mouths of a new generation that once again feels compelled to march in the streets of Harlem, Ferguson, and Baltimore. What Baldwin knew is that he left no heirs, he left spares, and that is why we carry him with us. So now when people ask me about James Baldwin, I tell them another truth: He is my brother, he ain't heavy.

Lonely in America

WENDY S. WALTERS

I have never been particularly interested in slavery, perhaps because it is such an obvious fact of my family's history. We know where we were enslaved in America, but we don't know much else about our specific conditions. The fact that I am descended from slaves is hard to acknowledge on a day-to-day basis, because slavery does not fit with my self-image. Perhaps this is because I am pretty certain I would not have survived it. I am naturally sharp-tongued, suffer from immobility when I am cold, and am susceptible to terrible sinus infections and allergies. My eyesight is poor. Most of the time I don't think about how soft the good fortune of freedom has made me, but if I were to quantify my weakness of body and character I would guess that at least half the fortitude my enslaved ancestors must have possessed has been lost with each generation in the family line, leaving me with little more than an obtuse and metaphorical relationship to that sort of suffering.

I resist thinking about slavery because I want to avoid the overwhelming feeling that comes from trying to conceive of the terror, violence, and indignity of it. I do not like to think of it happening in my hometown, where I work, in my neighborhood, or near any of the places where I conduct my life. My cultural memory of slavery, which I don't think is so unlike that of many other Americans, suggests that it was primarily a Southern phenomenon, one confined to the borders of plantations, which, if they haven't been transformed into shopping complexes or subdivisions, exist now only as nostalgic, sentimentalized tourist attractions. The landscapes associated with slavery, however, extend far beyond the South.

My home is in New England and in the winter my house feels slight against the wind as its windows tremble with every blustery gust, which makes me want to stay in bed, though I am not at all the type of person who likes to linger there once awake, unless circumstances are such that I am not alone, and then, even in that rare case, I can be restless and ready to set forth at sunrise. In the winter of 2006, I was not working at my regular job, which might have been a good thing had I not been prone to a melancholy obsession over recent personal disappointments. I began to notice pains in my body I had never felt before: a tendon pulling across the length of my leg when I sat down, a sharp twinge in my side when I stood up, and sometimes when I'd shower my skin was so sore I could barely stand to feel the water on it. I knew these pains were likely psychosomatic, evidence of how deeply I was suffering from loneliness. Because I suspected that the hope of escaping my loneliness was adding to my discomfort, I had been trying to cure myself of optimism as a strategy to ward off future misery. The value of this approach was confirmed by a self-help book I kept on my nightstand. When I dared to open it, I could read only a single chapter at a sitting because each reiterated a simple point that I just could not seem to accept—that to become free from disappointment one must acknowledge the obvious, then learn to live with it.

By mid-January, the United States' war with Iraq was coming to the end of its fourth year, the war in Afghanistan was intensifying again, and the shortcomings of the federal government that had been noted after Hurricane Katrina were fading from media attention, which was now absorbed with a surge of reports that, come summer, another movie star couple would be expecting their first biological child. I found myself momentarily enthralled in speculation: How long would this new relationship last? What did his ex-wife think of the sudden pregnancy of his new girlfriend? Who would take time off from their career to care for the family? These questions, though deeply irrelevant to my own life, served to distract me from the obvious fact that an unpopular war, entered into on misinformation, was showing no signs of ending. I studied the news reports on the radio every morning, which covered many subjects: planned highway construction projects, politics, movie stars, pop music stars, television stars, impending diseases, lying politicians, local sports, bank robberies, soldiers killed in Iraq. I suppose I was hoping the radio would serve as a kind of personal oracle, that stories of real human struggle might release me from solipsistic self-pity and show me how to leave my bungalow by entering the world with a sense of purpose, or at least a sense of direction.

It was with this ambition that I had gone to New Orleans to help my great-aunt Louise come to recognize that her home there had been destroyed, even though my gumption was clearly tainted with dread. Sitting in a cold house listening to the radio was painful enough, but the thought of actually walking through so much loss made me worry that I would have to face more of the obvious than I could be distracted from noticing. As our plane flew over the Gulf Coast it was hard to tell how bad things actually were on the ground. Muddy patches of brown and tan signaled the normally slow growth of a Southern winter. I saw the edge of Lake Pontchartrain, into which, during the early 1920s, my great-grandmother Susie had thrown her wedding ring when she needed to affirm a point that her husband would not accept. On our descent I began to see blue tarps stretched over large holes in people's roofs.

When we arrived at Aunt Lou's tiny red-brick, railroad-style house, her nephew met us. Chester was a former longshoreman. He had returned to the city a few weeks after the water had been pumped out and had been living in a FEMA trailer while he gutted his own house. Even though he had warned my mother and Aunt Lou on the phone that the house was in very bad condition, he wanted to make sure we understood this before we entered it, because from the outside, there appeared to be little structural damage. About four feet from the ground, a black, bathtub-ring-like watermark circled the exterior. Garbage and a broken ladder lay across the front lawn. When we opened the front door, dirt, mud, debris, and seaweed covered the hardwood floors and the sofa, which had floated over to the opposite wall from where it had been set. The house looked like someone had picked it up and shook it hard before setting it back down onto its cinder-block frame. We put on face masks and gloves, and booties over our shoes. A chifforobe sitting in water for weeks had gently exploded and still-wet clothes poked out of holes in the sides. Black and brown mud blotted the wall next to an antique brass bed. In the back room, the ceiling had caved in and wires and other debris hung low from what was left of the roof, like snakes in trees.

Aunt Lou said, *My house is tore up.*

Radio and television news reports about New Orleans mentioned that several of the city's cemeteries had been badly damaged by the flooding, and Chester's wife said coffins had been turning up all over the city. So I convinced my mother to drive over to Holt Cemetery, where our family crypt is situated, but she wouldn't get out of the car to check on it with me. Instead she shouted from its window, *Watch out for water moccasins!* as I walked through a rusty and twisted wrought-iron fence bolstered by rotten tree stumps into a field of tall, dead grasses and sun-bleached tombstones. Cypress trees sheltered the perimeter, branches reaching like veins across a heart.

Despite the fact that most of the graves at Holt are below-ground, unlike many cemeteries in New Orleans, it looked to me that Holt had kept hold of its dead better than the grave sites near the end of Canal Street, where mausoleums appeared stained and tumbled over by water. In the early 1900s a portion of Holt was used as a "pauper's field" for the poor and indigent, and during segregation it was one place where blacks could be buried. Our family crypt had been there longer than anyone could remember, but its precise location was unknown; its marker had been stolen in 1969, just weeks after my great-grandmother was laid to rest. Up close I could see new grass, slender and gold-green, appearing in short tufts at the foot of the headstones, most of which were pitched in one direction or another toward the ground. Handmade markers in wood or cement were adorned with bottle glass, sea shells, or not at all, with the names and dates of the deceased written in by hand. Some had been decorated with Mardi Gras beads and silk flowers. I walked down the dirt path to the part of the cemetery where most of the stones were missing and called out to my ancestors. *I have no idea where you are. Tell me where you are.* But I heard nothing.

Ten years ago, when I last visited Holt, the grounds had not been well tended, and even then many of the grave markers were missing, in disrepair, or toppled down. Back then I had only a piece of scrap paper with a row and plot number written on it to guide me to the crypt's location. The ground, deeply sunken where bodies were buried, looked as if waves were passing through it in slow motion. On that visit I worried that I could not read the names of the people I was walking over to apologize directly for the disrespect of having done so. Hastily I laid some flowers and a note where I thought the crypt should be and left without ever planning to return. On this visit, Holt felt strangely serene; unlike the rest of the city, it appeared not to have changed in any significant way. In fact, I might have wandered among the unknown dead for hours had I not heard my mother frantically shouting from the car. *Wendy, come on! We've got to get to Constantinople before dark!*

We picked up Aunt Lou from Chester's and drove over to Constantinople, a street in the Magazine district, to meet up with her childhood friend who had survived the flood trapped with her son in the attic of his house for a week before being rescued. Because none of the traffic lights were working, my mother was nervous and complained all the way there about how I had lingered too long in the cemetery. She chided me that one should let the dead rest. *That's right*, Aunt Lou said. I interrupted: *I just wanted to make sure that our people hadn't floated away.* They went quiet.

But I took a walk around, and it looked like everybody was still tucked in tight.

I returned from New Orleans more miserable than when I left. As much as I had wanted to come back from that trip with a sense of conviction, inspired to action that would distract me from my loneliness, I could not find a singular source of outrage on which to fixate—not poverty, racism, the failure of the federal government, a history of community self-destructiveness, a river, a lake, or a hurricane. Not a house without a roof, a felled tree across a path, a tumbled-down tombstone, or a wayward corpse. I was faced with too much that was obvious about the way class and race work in America. More than I wanted to see. More than I was capable of seeing.

This is when I realized my loneliness had deeper roots than I had initially suspected, and that, in addition to personal disappointments, it came from having a profound sense of disconnection from what I thought America was, and who, in that context, I knew myself to be. My post–New Orleans loneliness seemed to emanate from a place that preceded my own memory and stretched across time into a future that extended far beyond my vision. It was as if I had been thrown overboard into the sea and was paralyzed by the shock of it. I could neither breathe nor drown. I could not sink or return to the surface.

Then early one morning in January as I was listening to Boston's public radio station, I heard a story about the 2003 discovery of a grave site in Portsmouth, New Hampshire. As city workers attempted to dig a manhole near the corner of Court and Chestnut streets in the seaside town, a pine coffin was discovered with leg bones sticking out. An independent archaeological firm had been brought in immediately to lead an exhumation. Eight coffins and the remains of thirteen people were removed. The report noted that a combination of forensic evidence and DNA testing had confirmed that at least four of the remains in question were of African ancestry, most likely slaves buried there during the 1700s. The archaeologists' report had just been released to the city of Portsmouth, which was engaged in public discussion about the most appropriate and respectful way to deal with those exhumed, as well as the fact that as many as two hundred people might still be buried at the site.

Perhaps if I had not already spent more than a couple of weeks being so down in the dumps, if talk about the expected duration of the wars in Iraq and Afghanistan suggested a time frame other than the interminable, if images from my trip to New Orleans were not so powerfully present to me, then maybe the NPR report would have floated past me that morning. But something about hearing that Africans are buried beneath a public street in a small, coastal New England town gave me a new context to reconsider what is obvious and how one might learn to live with it. I knew I had to go there to see the people, even if they were still tucked in tight, if I was ever going to start letting go of the expectation that I could someday feel less lonely in America.

The first time I drove the two hours north from Providence to Portsmouth I had no idea what I was going to do when I got there. It was a Sunday in late February, the day after a large snowfall had dumped about six inches of snow along New England's southern coast. By morning, the roads were no longer wet and the snowdrifts at the side of the road glowed while ghostly wisps of fine powder swirled in the winnows of eighteen-wheelers trying to close the distance on Monday. From the interstate, I saw a sign for the Strawbery Banke Museum, which had been mentioned in the radio report, and I followed its direction.

The museum turned out to be a neighborhood of restored colonial houses at the edge of the Piscataqua River. The main entrance was closed, so I followed an elderly white couple into Stoodley's Tavern, which served as the museum ticket office on weekends. An older white woman with silver-bobbed hair sat at a table covered with pamphlets advertising local tourist attractions. *Are you here for the tour?* she asked. I nodded yes. *Ten dollars.* Charles, our docent, chatted about the weather with the five of us who waited for the tour to begin: me, the senior couple from Kittery, Maine, and a very young, blond couple just recently moved to Vermont from Tahoe, Nevada.

We walked across the street into the original settlement founded in 1630, known as Puddle Dock. The Old Mainer wanted to know: *Where were the borders of the marsh before the houses were built? Where had the water been pushed back to?* He was wearing a cap that said *USS Indianapolis.* Charles asked him if he was on the ship during WWII and he said yes. Charles said, *Were you on it when it went down?* The Old Mainer told us that he had gone ashore at Pearl Harbor just before the ship had set sail for Guam. Charles enthusiastically told us the story of how the ship went down, as if its history illuminated an unseen aspect of the tour. On July 30, 1945, the ship, en route from Guam to the Gulf of Leyte, was torpedoed by the Japanese. More than nine hundred sailors were hurled into cold, choppy water. Although they radioed U.S. forces for help as they went down, no one came for four days. By August 8, at the end of the rescue effort, only 317 men of the 1,196 originally on board had survived. The rest had been picked off by sharks or drowned.

After looking through a few of the houses in Puddle Dock, the Old Mainer, his wife, and I fell behind the guide and the young couple, who kept bragging about the beehive stove in an eighteenth-century farmhouse they were thinking of buying and restoring. They asked questions about the interior design of every home we toured. I took copious notes on Portsmouth's history and in this, felt my dour mood lightening. Details were comforting. Charles told us that Portsmouth was an Anglican, not Puritan, settlement and that among its original inhabitants were seventy-two Africans and eight Danes. Many of the wealthiest families in town made their fortunes in "the trade" first by shipping food, lumber, livestock, and other goods to British colonies in the West Indies and then by carrying captured Africans to the Caribbean, Virginia, and Portsmouth from the late seventeenth century through much of the eighteenth. Throughout the tour Charles occasionally used the word "servant" but never the word "slave."

In an alcove at the top of a staircase in a house built in 1790, the Old Mainer said to me, *I'd never live in one of these old houses. They're too cold.* There were two pictures on the mantel over the fireplace in the dining room. One called *An Emblem of Africa* featured a black woman walking with a feathered headdress next to a tiger in the background. The other picture, *An Emblem of Europe*, featured a white woman with a globe at her feet holding a book and a horn of plenty filled with fruit and flowers at the crook of her arm.

When the young couple asked about the role of the Native population in the development of Portsmouth, Charles explained that they were not a factor: *Most died out before the town became sizable, after catching diseases from their contact with the Europeans*, he said.

At the end of the tour, I returned to Stoodley's Tavern to ask for directions to the slave graves mentioned in the radio report. Charles told me, *You can't see anything. There's nothing there.* I thought he meant that the site had not been commemorated or officially rededicated, but his reaction made me wonder if there was even a historical marker indicating the graveyard's boundaries. The woman who had sold me a ticket said, *They've been reinterred.* I told them I still planned to go and asked if Chestnut Street was close, since Portsmouth's downtown area is quite small. *Or should I drive?* I said. She responded tersely, *It doesn't matter. It's just an intersection.*

It was sharply cold and the wind was picking up when I arrived at Chestnut Street near the corner of Court. Several restored colonials now serving as lawyers' and doctors' offices lined its east side. On the west side there was a beauty salon and a sign indicating a "Drug Free School Zone." Other than these buildings, it seemed that there *was* nothing to see. As I rounded the corner at Chestnut and State, I noticed a brass plaque affixed to the clapboards of a house: *In colonial Portsmouth, segregation applied in death as in life. City officials approved a plan in 1705 that set aside this city block for a 'Negro Burial Ground.' It was close to town but pushed to what was then its outer edge. By 1813, houses were built over the site.* I got back in my car to write notes about what I found. This is when I realized my car was probably sitting on top of people. I knew I should feel something about that, but all I felt was a familiar loneliness creeping in on me.

The trip to Portsmouth had not elicited much outrage in me, even after I discovered that one of the oldest known grave sites of blacks in New England was neither green nor sacred space. I accepted the reality that the historic colonial houses—now the business residences of attorneys, hairstylists, insurance agents, and doctors—were considered by most people to be more valuable than the bodies down below them. But while I had thought that my lack of feelings while standing on people would allow me to forget that I had been standing on people, it didn't. I had no intuition about how these dead Africans might have felt about being paved over, no feelings of ancestral connection to those buried below, and I heard no discernible voices calling to me from the depths of that darkness. I wondered if the woman at the museum had been right. Maybe the corner *was* just an intersection.

The ambivalence the folks at the Strawbery Banke Museum expressed for those buried beneath Portsmouth's downtown was all the more surprising when I later learned that the first bodies exhumed from the African Burying

Ground had been housed at the museum before they were transported to the temporary laboratory. I assumed that my own lack of feeling was due, in part, to the randomness with which I had selected Portsmouth as the place to try to make sense of the remains of slavery in America. I had no personal connection to New Hampshire, no familial bond to any of the people buried there, and I became certain that was the reason I couldn't feel anything while standing on those Africans. I thought maybe I needed to visit a slave grave site more closely related to my life if I was going to experience some true cathexis.

So once back in Rhode Island, I went to a talk given by Theresa Guzmán Stokes at Newport's Redwood Library about that city's largest African burial ground, called God's Little Acre, a cemetery founded in 1747. For more than twenty years, without city support, she had been maintaining its grounds out of personal respect for those buried there, clearing away litter and weeds and eventually establishing a fund to protect it. She runs a website about the cemetery, and she and her husband, Keith Stokes, former executive director of the Newport County Chamber of Commerce, are writing a book on the subject.

While introducing his wife, Stokes assured the small audience, *We're not interested in slavery. It's emotional and it separates people.* But the absurdity of slavery means it is practically impossible for anyone to contain all the contradictions that arise when speaking of it. So despite his promise seconds earlier to refrain from talk of slavery, Stokes started by explaining how often the term "servant" is used as a euphemism for "slave" in New England and how there is a presumption that Africans here were somehow "smarter" and treated better than those in the South. *This misperception*, he pushed, *is because people don't want to remember the dehumanization.* Without hesitating, he went on to say, *Slavery is violent, grotesque, vulgar, and we are all implicated in how it denigrates humanity.*

According to a series of articles by Paul Davis running that same week in the *Providence Journal*, Newport was a hugely significant port in the North Atlantic slave trade, and from 1725 to 1807 more than a thousand trips were made to Africa in which more than a hundred thousand men, women, and children were forced into slavery in the West Indies and throughout the American colonies. Ms. Guzmán Stokes explained how African people built many of the prominent colonial houses throughout New England, including those in Newport, and while many of those buildings remain restored in one form or another, just a handful of graves of Africans who made this contribution to the town's development can be found.

On my way to God's Little Acre, I came upon the tiny Newport Historical Cemetery #9, which Theresa Guzmán Stokes had also mentioned during her talk, but I could not figure out which graves belonged to Africans and which belonged to whites. A white woman was taking pictures of stones, so I asked her if she knew. She pointed to two graves in the corner. *These over here*, she said and then explained she had looked for information on African graves on the Web before she left her home in Seattle. The woman told me she was originally from Connecticut, but when she decided to marry an African American man in the 1970s, her family disowned her. She had four children with him, none of whom ever met her parents. She had brought her youngest daughter back east to visit historical sites for a vacation and confessed that she was glad she no longer lived in New England. *I couldn't take all of this "in your face" history. Like Thames Street, the blue stones*, she said, referring to the pavers on a road that edges Newport's harbor. *Each one of those stones represents an African. Every stone was from the ballast of a slave ship and was carried by a slave as he or she debarked.* When I called the Newport Historical Society to confirm this, the reference librarian and genealogist Bert Lippincott III, C.G., insisted that stones like that were used as ballast on all ships coming into Newport, not just slave ships. He added, *Many Newporters bankrolled ships in the trade, but Newport was not a major destination for slave ships.* When I mentioned the article in the *Providence Journal* that claimed most Africans in colonial Newport were slaves, he said, *Many were third-generation Americans. Most were skilled, literate, and worked as house servants.*

At God's Little Acre on the edge of Newport, three stones stand erect, three others appear jackknifed into the ground at a forty-five-degree angle. One lies level to the ground. Only these seven tombstones remain in the graveyard that commemorates the contributions of Africans to the city's early history. While surrounded on three sides by larger, crowded cemeteries and an eight-foot wrought-iron fence facing Farewell Street, God's Little Acre is comparatively pastoral, and most of the grave markers are missing as a result of vandalism or landscaping contractors running tractor mowers through it for many years. The inscriptions on those few slate stones still standing are fading due to the way weather and pollution wear on them. Many are now just barely legible.

A white woman with a backpack was taking pictures of the scant stones. She told me she teaches courses on American graveyards at a school in Connecticut. Pointing to one of the graves, she said, *He must have been loved by his "family" because stones were very expensive back then.* I wanted to say, *So were people.* And then I remembered reading an inventory from the estate of Joseph Sherburne, whose house has been preserved at the Strawbery Banke Museum. The linens were listed as worth forty dollars while the African woman who washed and pressed them had a line-item value of fifty dollars.

My trip to Newport made me realize that I knew almost nothing about the lives of blacks in Portsmouth during slavery and I wondered if *that* was the reason I was so unmoved by my visit. So I drove back up to New Hampshire to walk the Black Heritage Trail, put together by a retired schoolteacher and local historian, Valerie Cunningham, in order to learn about the experiences of Africans and African Americans in Portsmouth. Some of the sites on the Black Heritage Trail highlight historic accomplishments of blacks in

Portsmouth such as the *New Hampshire Gazette* printing office where Primus, a skilled slave, operated a press for fifty years; the Town Pump and Stocks, where black leaders were elected in a ritual following loosely from the Ashanti festival tradition of Odwira; and St. John's Church, where the records indicate that Venus, most likely a poor but free black woman, received a gift of one dollar from the church in 1807 on Christmas Day.

I sat on a bench overlooking the Memorial Bridge, which crosses the Piscataqua River from Kittery, Maine, to where captive Africans would have first encountered Portsmouth, the wharf at what is now Prescott Park. The first known African captive arrived in Portsmouth around 1645 from Guinea, and slave ships started landing regularly as early as 1680 carrying small loads of mostly male children and adolescents. I tried to imagine what it felt like to come into this swiftly moving river harbor after a long journey across the Atlantic in the cargo hold of a ship—after having been starved, beaten, shackled, and covered in the feculence of the living and dead. Did seeing the flat, tidy fronts of buildings outlining this colonial settlement for the first time make them feel hopeful? So many rectangles. How far away the rest of the world must have seemed.

I ended my walk at the Portsmouth Public Library, which held no significance on the trail, but, according to the first news story I heard about the burial ground, had in its collection a copy of the archaeologists' report on the burial site.

When I asked a reference librarian if I could see it, she hesitated and wanted to know if I planned on making copies. I told her I was not sure if I wanted to make copies because I hadn't yet seen the report. She then consulted with the head reference librarian, who told me that the burial site is a very sensitive issue for the city and that he needed to consult with the city attorney's office before releasing it. He took down my information—name, city of residence, and school affiliation—then asked me to wait while he placed the call.

The librarian was worried about how I might represent Portsmouth in a piece on the subject, because he cared about the town. I liked the town, too. It is pretty, easy to navigate, and surprisingly friendly for New England. I felt guilty and ashamed about my affinity for the town because at the time I could not muster more than a diffuse intellectual identification with the people who were buried just a few streets over.

Before copying the report, I remembered how easy it was for me to ignore what was already obvious, so I wrote down some details to remind myself of what I shouldn't forget: people were carried like chattel on ships to America; they were sold to other people; they were stripped of their names, spiritual practices, and culture; they worked their entire lives without just compensation; they were beaten into submission and terrorized or killed if they chose not to submit; when they died they were buried in the ground at the far edge of town; and as the town grew, roads and houses were built on top of them as if they had never existed.

I spent the long summer with my friends at the beach,

drinking Bloody Marys and eating lobster rolls on the open-air deck of a clam shack in Galilee, Rhode Island, while the Block Island Ferry, serried with tourists, made its lethargic heave past the docked commercial fishing boats. Once school started, I turned my attention back to the spiritless tedium of lesson planning and grading papers. In all that time I did not once touch the archaeologists' report.

I could make something up about why I let the report sit in a manila folder on my desk for nine months without ever once attempting to read it—something about wanting to let the dead rest or about how loneliness swells and recedes—but I won't. The reason is not clear to me even now. What I do know is that holding the copy I had made of the report near the Xerox machine by the dimly lit front door of the Portsmouth Public Library that previous spring made me feel more than I had felt during any of my grave-site visits, like a balloon in my chest was expanding and taking up all the space I normally used to breathe.

Intense discomfort, I had thought. *Maybe that's enough.*

But by January I was driving back up to Portsmouth, irritated with myself for not reading the copy of the report I had already made but even more irritated with myself for not being able to let it go unread. The once tattered and gloomy public library had moved to a brilliant new building a few streets over, and as I walked around the landscapers installing the brick steps, I caught the sign on the door that said, "Welcome to Your New Library." In the breezeway, three junior high school girls gathered around a computer terminal and giggled. A woman in a purple cardigan greeted me from behind the circulation desk with a smile and thin wave. Seduced by all of it, I thought, *I love my new library.*

When I asked the reference librarian about the report, he told me it was now shelved in the local history section in the regular stacks. I thought, *Now it's all out in the open. Now there's nothing to hide.* I grabbed it off the wall, took a seat at one of the new blond reading tables, and thumbed through it lightly as if it were a mere tabloid magazine. I took notes from the acknowledgments, introduction, and background chapters, but when I got to the section describing the removal of the coffins—those same pages I had copied nearly a year before—a shrill noise came up from the back of my throat at the pitch of a full teakettle in a rolling-boil whistle. I cleared my throat and went back to reading, but my din started again. It was sharp enough for anyone to hear, so I decided I had better leave—but not before making a fresh copy of the report to take with me.

When a story is unpleasant, it is hard to focus on details that allow you to put yourself in the place of the subject, because the pain of distortion starts to feel familiar. Paying attention often requires some sort of empathy for the subject, or at the very least, for the speaker. But empathy, these days, is hard to come by. Maybe this is because everyone is having such a hard time being understood themselves. Or because empathy requires us to dig way down into the murk, deeper than our own feelings go, to a place where the boundaries between our experience and everyone else's no longer exist.

Archaeologists removed the remains of thirteen people from beneath the intersection of Chestnut and State streets with the help of some machinery, but they did most of the digging by hand. Once in the laboratory, they used potters' tools and paintbrushes to remove excess soil from the bones and teeth. The exact dates associated with each burial remain unknown, but it is assumed that all were interred during the eighteenth century. Four males and one female could be identified by sex, but they found it impossible to determine the sex of the other eight, though most were believed to be in early adulthood, between the ages of twenty-one and forty years. Heads of the deceased generally faced west, suggesting a burial in the Christian tradition. In no cases were all the bones of an individual represented, perhaps due to the commingling of remains during previous installations of gas and sewer lines, the stacking of coffins, or a high water table in the soil. Thus no cause of death could be determined for any of those recovered. Archaeologists noted, however, that the lack of visible traumatic defects, cut marks, fresh or healed fractures does not rule out the presence of trauma. The teeth of each person, which in several cases constituted the entirety of the remains, appeared to be better preserved than their bones, which were found wet, free of flesh, colored gray or black, and, in the case of long bones, often missing the ends.

Pieces of the skull, portions of the upper and lower limbs, shoulder girdle, ribs, spine, and pelvis of a male person between the ages of twenty-one and thirty years represent Burial 1. An excavator operator noticed his leg bones sticking out from the bottom of his coffin, which was made of white pine and was hexagonal in shape. All of his mandibular and some of his maxillary teeth were present, but like most of those recovered at the site, his teeth exhibited traces of enamel hypoplasia, a sign of previous infection or nutritional stress. His bones revealed a calcified blood vessel in his right lower leg and prolonged shin splints. A pumpkin seed of unexplained significance was found in his coffin as well as a metal object, probably a shroud pin, suggesting he was naked at burial.

In Burial 2, the remains of another male person between twenty-one and twenty-six years of age were found in good condition despite the fact that part of his skull had been unintentionally crushed by the excavator, leaving only his mandible and several teeth. A gas line running through the foot portion of his coffin meant that many bones in his right foot also were missing. His body was slumped to the left side, probably due to his coffin being tipped during burial, and his hipbone was broken in several places. His right hand lay over his thigh. Further analysis of his bones showed signs of repetitive forearm rotation and possible inflammation of the right leg, presumably from heavy shoveling, lifting, or other strenuous work. Salt, either used as a preservative before burial or for some other ritual, and a single tooth of unknown origin found between his knees, further distinguished his remains.

Burial 3 contained the remains of a person of indeterminate sex, thought to be approximately thirty to fifty years of age with the head facing east, perhaps toward Mecca.

Archaeologists recovered only extremely fragile fragments of the cranium and major long bones. The part of the mandible that was still intact suggests participation in a West African puberty ritual as there is a long-healed-over gap where lower and lateral incisors would have been. Stains in the soil represented most of the coffin wood. Only thirty teeth, small fragments of bone, some twenty wood and coffin nails accounted for the person of twenty-one to forty years of age in Burial 4. Those remains were extremely damaged by erosion and the unintentional intrusion of the excavator.

Pipe laid around 1900 across the bottom of the coffin of the male person aged twenty-one to forty in Burial 5 eventually disintegrated his lower extremities. Shovel marks on the coffin base indicate where a crew member either hit his coffin accidentally or attempted to cut through it.

The head of the female person in Burial 6 was located under the sidewalk, which had to be caved in to allow for her removal. Only the upper portion of her coffin was found intact. Her lower legs, cut off where they intersected with a utility trench and a ceramic sewage pipe installed around 1900, revealed evidence of a bone infection and severe inflammation of the shins. Her left arm appeared to be laid across her torso, and her cranium, now missing the face, pointed to the right side of the coffin. Her upper central incisors were shaved, possibly according to a West African cultural tradition, and represent the earliest documented case of such dental modification in North America.

The person in Burial 7 was a child between the ages of seven and twelve, of unknown sex, whose remains were damaged by heavy rain and a redirected sewer line that flooded the grave shaft during excavation. Decades of a sewer pipe lying across the child's midsection also contributed to this poor state, despite the fact that the coffin was found to be in relatively good condition. Directly beneath that body were the remains of a male person between twenty-one and forty years of age in Burial 12 whose bones were very soft also due to the high water table of the soil. At present, it is impossible to tell if these two people were buried at the same time or possibly even generations apart. The coffinless remains of persons in Burials 2B, 3B, 4B, 5B, and 7B were discovered beneath the sidewalk. Dental fragments and hand bones from a person not presently attributed to Burial 2 but found nearby are all that exists of the person in Burial 2B. Twelve teeth represent the person in Burial 3B. One tooth each indicates persons in Burials 4B and 5B, and a femur shaft fragment resting atop the child's coffin in Burial 7 is all that was found of the person in Burial 7B.

The boundaries of Portsmouth's African Burying Ground are still a mystery, as they have been for more than one hundred years, but plans to build a formal memorial are under way. Public discussions led by the state's archaeologists have asked city residents to consider whether a part of either street should be closed to vehicular traffic. Some Portsmouth residents have submitted samples of their DNA to see if they are in any way related to those people whose remains, now stored in Ethafoam, 0.002 mil polybags, and acid-free archival storage boxes in a municipally provided laboratory space, await reinterment.

Because I worried that I would lose track of the archaeologists' report among the bills, magazines, and student papers that littered my desk, for many months I kept it beside my bed, on the floor beneath my nightstand. Each morning the radio woke me with news of the war, a pop star's addiction, dismal predictions for the American economy. Later, I put the report in my backpack, its pages flat against my spine. At some point, I am not sure when, I grew accustomed to its weight and stopped noticing I was carrying it around.

Where Do We Go from Here?

ISABEL WILKERSON

Before the summer of 2014, before we had seen Eric Garner dying on a Staten Island street and Michael Brown lifeless in the Missouri sun for hours, before the grand jury decisions and the die-ins that shut down interstates, we may have lulled ourselves into believing that the struggle was over, that it had all been taken care of back in 1964, that the marching and bloodshed had established, once and for all, the basic rights of people who had been at the bottom for centuries. We may have believed that, if nothing else, the civil rights movement had defined a bar beneath which we could not fall.

But history tells us otherwise. We seem to be in a continuing feedback loop of repeating a past that our country has yet to address. Our history is one of spectacular achievement (as in black senators of the Reconstruction era or the advances that culminated in the election of Barack Obama) followed by a violent backlash that threatens to erase the gains and then a long, slow climb to the next mountain, where the cycle begins again.

The last reversal of black advancement was so crushing that historians called it the Nadir. It followed the leaps

African Americans made after enslavement, during the cracked window of opportunity known as Reconstruction. The newly freed people built schools and businesses and ascended to high office.

But a conservative counterreaction led to a gutting of the civil rights laws of that time and to the start of a Jim Crow caste system in the South that restricted every step an African American could make. Any breach of the system could mean one's life. African Americans were lynched over accusations of mundane infractions, such as stealing a hog or 75 cents, during a period that lasted into the 1940s.

Six million African Americans fled that caste system, seeking asylum in the rest of the country during what would become the Great Migration. Denied the ballot, they voted with their bodies.

Their defection put pressure on the country, North and South, and freed them to pursue their dreams of self-determination. But in the North, they were met with hostility from the onset—redlining, overpolicing, hyper-segregation, the seeds of the disparities we see today. The past few months have forced us to confront our place in a country where we were enslaved for far longer than we have been free. Forced us to face the dispiriting erosion that we have witnessed in recent years—from the birther assaults on a sitting black president to the gutting of the Voting Rights Act that we had believed was carved in granite.

And now police assaults on black people for the most ordinary human behaviors—a father tasered in Minnesota while waiting for his children; a motorist shot to death in

North Carolina while seeking help after a car accident. It is as if we have reentered the past and are living in a second Nadir: It seems the rate of police killings now surpasses the rate of lynchings during the worst decades of the Jim Crow era. There was a lynching every four days in the early decades of the twentieth century. It's been estimated that an African American is now killed by police every two to three days.

The outcomes in Staten Island and Ferguson and elsewhere signal, as in the time of Jim Crow, that the loss of black life at the hands of authorities does not so much as merit further inquiry and that the caste system has only mutated with the times. From this, we have learned that the journey is far from over and that we must know our history to gain strength for the days ahead. We must love ourselves even if—and perhaps especially if—others do not. We must keep our faith even as we work to make our country live up to its creed. And we must know deep in our bones and in our hearts that if the ancestors could survive the Middle Passage, we can survive anything.

"The Dear Pledges of Our Love":
A Defense of Phillis Wheatley's Husband*

HONORÉE FANONNE JEFFERS

As a little girl in the seventies, I memorized the names of prominent African Americans for Black History Month. These were the images that my teachers would trace from construction paper, then tack to the bulletin boards in my school. How I loved those dark silhouettes.

My school was 99 percent segregated; the laws had changed in the South but custom had not. My teachers celebrated black "firsts" to shore up our self-esteem, to fortify us against our smaller and shabbier schools and a pervasive white unfriendliness from those outside our enclave.

To my teachers, the eighteenth-century poet Phillis Wheatley was the *first* of the firsts, a beacon for black children. My parents were teachers, too, and at home they filled in the details. Wheatley was a child stolen from across the Atlantic and enslaved. A young genius whose playthings were the poems of Homer and Terence, she was the first

---

*The title of this essay uses a line from Phillis Wheatley's "To a Clergyman on the Death of His Lady," published in *Poems on Various Subjects, Religious and Moral* (1773).

African woman on this side of the Atlantic to publish a book of poetry. Neither of my parents liked her poetry much, but that wasn't the point. The point was loyalty to the race, to African American men and women. This probably wasn't my first lesson about the responsibilities of being a black person, but it's the first one I remember and the most lasting.

I don't recall my elementary school teachers or my parents ever mentioning Wheatley's husband. I believed she never had married before dying at the young age of thirty-four, and I found it heartbreaking that she did not have someone to love from her native land, someone who looked like her and shared the same cultural memories. All she had was the white people who used to own her. When I first encountered information about Wheatley's husband, John Peters, in my junior year of college, I was confronted with the dominant negative stereotypes of black men. Those thirty-five words describe him as an arrogant good-for-nothing who deserted his family.

Talladega College, where I was studying at the time, was founded by former slaves. The campus is situated in a rural Alabama town, but smack in the middle of the 'hood. As I read the words portraying Peters, how he had abandoned Wheatley and their children, leaving them to poverty and then eventual death in the midst of squalor, images of black men came to me: the shiftless brothers who hung at the edge of campus, townies waiting for college girls. They sometimes shouted to us and promised pleasures of all kinds. These were the young men my doggedly middle-class mother had warned me about, in her alto, cigarette-tuned voice. My mother had fought her way up from backwoods poverty in rural Georgia and she cautioned me: One wrong step with a man could land me in perdition; living in a shack or a one-room apartment surrounded by my screaming, misbehaved progeny. As a formerly poor person, my mother looked down her nose at poor, black folk who had not escaped to tell the advisory tale, as she had.

I thought of Wheatley, the "Ethiop" genius, taken in by Peters's charms, falling from her magnificent perch. I pictured her, beguiled by a man who whispered in her ear, told her lies to get into her starched, Good Negro bloomers.

Much of the information on Wheatley's personal life comes from *Memoir and Poems of Phillis Wheatley, A Native African and a Slave*, a book published in 1834, fifty years after the poet's death. The author, Margaretta Matilda Odell, identifies herself as a "collateral descendant" of Phillis's former mistress. In her biography of Wheatley, she pushes a well-meaning abolitionist message: Black folks do not deserve to be slaves, and someone like Wheatley is the example of what her brethren could be, if they only had a chance.

According to Odell, the child-who-would-be-renamed-Phillis was "supposed to have been about seven years old, at this time, from the circumstance of shedding her front teeth" when she arrived in Boston. Susannah Wheatley, the wife of a merchant, was looking for a "faithful domestic in her old age." Instead, she found "the poor, naked child" with a piece of cloth tied around her like a skirt. Once the child was taken home,

> A daughter of Mrs. Wheatley, not long after the child's first introduction to the family, undertook to learn her to read and write; and, while she astonished her instructress by her rapid progress, she won the good will of her kind mistress, by her amiable disposition and the propriety of her behavior.

And with the help of Susannah, the smart and well-behaved Phillis began writing poetry. Odell doesn't give specific dates about Phillis's journey to freedom, but later biographers of the poet do. On May 8, 1773, she sailed to London (accompanied by the Wheatleys' grown son, Nathaniel) to promote her work, staying there six weeks. According to Wheatley scholar Vincent Carretta, on September 9, 1773, advertisements appeared for Phillis's only book of poetry, *Poems on Various Subjects, Religious and Moral.* We know that upon her return from London, her owners freed her, because Phillis mentions this fact in a letter dated October 18, 1773.

We can't know if Phillis hoped to return to her African homeland after receiving her freedom, but we do know that she retained a connection to the continent and its people. She developed a years-long friendship with Obour Tanner, a fellow kidnapped African who lived in Newport, Rhode Island. For several years, these two women exchanged fervent, spiritual thoughts in their letters. Phillis dedicated a poem to "S.M., A Young African Painter," and she references Africa in several of her poems, too. "To the Right Honorable William, Earl of Dartmouth" contains lines about her involuntary—and possibly violent—migration from her native land:

> Should you, my lord, while you peruse my song,
> Wonder from whence my love of Freedom sprung,
> Whence flow these wishes for the common good,
> By feeling hearts alone best understood,
> I, young in life, by seeming cruel fate
> Was snatch'd from Afric's fancy'd happy seat:
> What pangs excruciating must molest,
> What sorrows labour in my parent's breast?

Odell paints the Wheatleys as kind masters, and draws an especially sympathetic portrait of Susannah, who acted as an eighteenth-century stage mother to push forward Phillis's career. Susannah wrote to Selina, Countess of Huntingdon, a philanthropist and a leader in the Methodist movement, in an attempt to secure her patronage for the young poet. (The countess replied to this letter on May 13, 1773.) Phillis herself speaks lovingly of Susannah, and she continued to live with the Wheatleys after receiving her freedom. In a letter to Obour (dated March 21, 1774), Phillis writes of the death of her former mistress, and how a white woman treated Phillis as less a "servant" and more a "child." But as we look back on this era, kindness must be viewed through a complex prism, for slavery was a scatological, morally bankrupt enterprise. Besides Phillis, the Wheatleys owned at least one other slave and they did not raise their voices publicly or act overtly against the institution of slavery. Odell seems to think that Phillis was living the kidnapped African's dream, however, and that, after the death of Susannah, that dream collapsed:

At this period of destitution, Phillis received an offer of marriage from a respectable colored man of Boston. The name of this individual was Peters. He kept a grocery in Court-Street, and was a man of very handsome person and manners; wore a wig, carried a cane, and quite acted out "the gentleman." In an evil hour he was accepted; and he proved utterly unworthy of the distinguished woman who honored him by her alliance. He was unsuccessful in business, and failed soon after their marriage; and he is said to have been both too proud and too indolent to apply himself to any occupation below his fancied dignity. Hence his unfortunate wife suffered much from this ill-omened union.

Having written in great, flattering detail about the poet's years with the white Wheatleys, Odell uses her talents to draw a contemptuous likeness of John Peters. She informs us that Phillis never used the last name of her husband—and, it's implied, we should assume that this decision had something to do with Peters's qualities as a mate. Odell accuses him of possible abuse, writing in delicate terms that while Phillis was in very bad health, she wouldn't have been "unmindful . . . of her conjugal or matronly duties." In other words, Peters pressed his frail wife into sexual service when he shouldn't have, which resulted in (according to

Odell) three pregnancies. From there, Odell opines, Wheatley's destruction was a foregone conclusion: There was terrible poverty. Each of the three children born to Wheatley fell sick in infancy and died. And at the age of thirty-three or -four, Wheatley herself died from an illness exacerbated by her "extreme misery" in living in "a filthy apartment" with a "negligent" husband.

This is the story branded into literary history.

In 2003, while working on my third book of poetry, I read an essay on Wheatley written by Henry Louis Gates, Jr., in *The New Yorker*. It was an excerpt from his soon-to-be-published book, a treatment of Wheatley juxtaposed against the racism of Enlightenment scholars such as Immanuel Kant, and more specifically, Thomas Jefferson. As someone who explored American history in my poetry, I found Gates's thesis fascinating: He believed Wheatley was important in dispelling derisive eighteenth-century notions about black humanity; her poetry had rebutted Kant's ordering of the nations with Africans down at the very bottom. Because of Wheatley's important symbolism for black humanity, Thomas Jefferson's negative response to Wheatley's poetry—"[t]he compositions published under her name are below the dignity of criticism"—was a symbol as well. It meant that the struggle for black equality on all fronts was not yet won. And thus, Gates argues, an intellectual movement was born, one that triggered a wave of eighteenth-century black literary and scholarly production, which persisted into the 1960s and continues into contemporary times.

My encounter with Gates's article started me on a Wheatley reading jag. For the next six years, I read everything I could find on her. I checked books out from the library, I downloaded scholarly articles, and I began to think deeply about her most (in)famous poem, "On Being Brought from Africa to America." This eight-line poem begins with discordancy, with seeming racial self-hatred combined with religious fervor. The tone of these verses earned Wheatley sharp, ugly criticism from other black poets, most notably the Black Arts Movement poet Amiri Baraka (né LeRoi Jones):

'Twas mercy brought me from my *Pagan* land,
Taught my benighted soul to understand
That there's a God, that there's a *Saviour* too:
Once I redemption neither sought nor knew.

As a woman in my (then) thirties, I had a different take from Baraka. I thought about a little girl's pain at being torn from her parents in Africa, her trauma on board a slave ship. I thought of her mother's grief, her wondering what had become of her child. I thought about my own and other black folks' beliefs in a benevolent God, in spite of our history in this country, the brutality enacted against us. And in a burst of empathy, I wrote these lines:

Mercy: what Phillis claimed
after that sea journey.

Journey.
Let's call it that.

Let's lie to each other.

Not early descent into madness.
Naked travail among filth and rats.

What got Phillis over the sea?
What kept a stolen daughter?

Perhaps it was *mercy*,
Dear Reader.

Mercy,
Dear Brethren.

However, until I traveled to Worcester, Massachusetts, to the American Antiquarian Society, I had no idea that the devastating picture of the naked, gap-toothed child wrapped in a carpet may have been Odell's imaginary reflection. It was 2009, and I was the recipient of the society's artist fellowship. Its archives house one of the largest collections of printed material from early colonial days through 1876, about the United States, the West Indies, and Canada. I was on a mission to write a series of poems based upon Wheatley's life, and I was in search of primary resources.

At the beginning of my fellowship, I was ready to get to work. Though I'd been conducting archival research for nearly twenty years, I wasn't formally trained as a historian, but as the research librarians remarked, I was quick and a self-starter. In only a matter of days, I found references to Odell's *Memoir and Poems of Phillis Wheatley, A Native African and a Slave.* Looking through the bibliographies in texts on Wheatley, I noticed that they either cited *Memoir* directly or they summarized Odell and listed a relative of the Wheatley family as a reference. There was no overt tracing of Odell's lineage, no proof of how she was related to the Wheatleys, no way to establish Odell's authority.

In July, around the middle of my fellowship term, I drove from Worcester to the Northeast National Archives in Waltham, Massachusetts. It was at the urging of my mentor at the society that I made the drive, even after she told me that records would be on microfiche; the very mention of microfiche made me sick to my stomach. I spent a couple hours looking through the census records, and as I feared, it was not the exhilarating process I'd hoped for. My eyeballs ached and the lobster roll from the day before threatened to repeat on me.

I was ready to return to Worcester, when I saw John Peters on the 1790 census of Suffolk County, Massachusetts—the city of Boston. He was listed as a free man of color.

No, it wasn't a mistake. There was Peters's name.

Swallowing my nausea, I rechecked the entire census, just to be sure. There was no other black John Peters, the narcissistic man who had abandoned his wife off and on, and then—as Odell had written—supposedly had moved farther south after his wife's death. I looked the census over completely two more times and took pictures of the relevant pages.

I sat there, confused. Rather than verifying facts about America's first black poet, which had been my intention, I realized literary history had entrusted the story of Wheatley and Peters to a white woman who may have made assumptions about Wheatley's husband that might not just be wrong, but also the product of racial stereotypes.

Why *would* Peters have moved farther south after the Revolution? This piece of it didn't make sense to me. Why would a free, black man in his natural, right mind move south, taking his body to slaveholding territory, where white men would be waiting to place him in chains?

Wheatley had died in 1784, but the census had been taken in 1790. It's possible, then, that Peters had been in Boston through that decade, which meant that Peters may have been in Boston when Wheatley died. What could this mean? Had the young couple been separated? Had he left her for another woman? Had she left him? Maybe they had remained together. Maybe he hadn't abandoned her. Maybe Odell misrepresented their relationship. And if Odell had misrepresented the relationship of Wheatley and Peters, maybe she had done the same about her relationship to the white Wheatleys.

I drove back to the AAS and huddled with my mentor and the research librarian. I asked them what Odell meant in her book when she claimed to be a "collateral descendant" of the white Wheatleys? A cousin? A niece? An in-law married to a direct descendant? Both of them advised me to look up Odell in the New England Historic Genealogical Society. I did, and I found Margaretta Matilda Odell of "Jamaica Plain, Massachusetts"—and that's all I found. Nothing else.

I returned to the texts on Wheatley. In each, I double-checked the notes and indexes several times, sure that I had overlooked something. Every night, back in my fellow's room, I took hours to draft possible genealogies of the blood relatives and in-laws of Susannah and John Wheatley, and those of their twins, Mary Wheatley Lathrop and Nathaniel Wheatley. I uncovered no documentation connecting Odell to the white Wheatleys. There was no establishment of family bona fides. Rather, it appeared that the only proof that Odell had been related to Susannah Wheatley, the former mistress of Phillis Wheatley, was that *she had said so*.

Vincent Carretta, the author of *Phillis Wheatley: Biography of a Genius in Bondage* (2011)—to date, the most comprehensive biography of the poet—has unearthed a treasure trove of previously unpublished material on Phillis Wheatley and her husband: legal documents, newspaper notices, records in Boston's *Taking Book*, along with other important minutiae. Still, even Carretta doesn't know how or when Wheatley met Peters. There is a reference to a "young man" in a letter she wrote her friend Obour, on October 30, 1773, but we don't know his identity. We do know that in 1778, Phillis Wheatley and John Peters, "free Negroes," married during the tumultuous period of the American Revolution. In a letter to Obour (dated May 10, 1779), the poet signs herself as "Phillis Peters"; thereafter, whenever she refers to herself in print, she always uses her married name.

In the years leading up to the Revolution and directly afterward, Massachusetts was the site of black political agitation. Just as I had heard the name of Phillis Wheatley in elementary school, so had I learned about Crispus Attucks, a biracial African American and the first to fall during what became known as the Boston Massacre. Over the years, I would learn the names of others, like Lemuel Haynes, a minister who had fought in the Revolution, and Prince Hall, who founded the African Masons. There was Belinda, who petitioned the Massachusetts Assembly for a pension in her old age. And I would read the words of Felix, an unidentified black man—and presumably a slave—who petitioned the same body, demanding his freedom and that of other African American men:

> We have no Property. We have no Wives. No Children. We have no City. No Country. But we have a Father in Heaven, and we are determined, as far as his Grace shall enable us, and as far as our degraded contemptuous Life will admit, to keep all his Commandments. . . .

When I view Peters through the lens of the eighteenth century, he fits in quite easily with his brethren. Carretta depicts him as a smart, hard worker, trying his hand in different business enterprises: law, commerce, real estate, even medicine. (The latter was not the profession that we know today, and required no specific schooling.)

As a white woman of the nineteenth century Odell fits in perfectly with her era, too. It doesn't take much speculation to deduce that she believed Peters to be an uppity Negro. He was a black man who had the nerve to possess high self-esteem, who cajoled Wheatley away from her white friends. Even though Odell dedicates her book to "friends of the Africans," her tone ridicules his ambitions: "[Peters] is said to have been both too proud and too indolent to apply himself to any occupation below his fancied dignity." In other words, how dare a black man want to be anything other than a day laborer with calluses on his hands? Who did he think he was, to desire property and not *be* property, to style himself as a business owner, to marry a high-status, accomplished woman of his own race?

There are other second- or third-hand, derisive accounts of Wheatley's husband, all by whites. Carretta quotes from Josiah Quincy, who claims to have met John Peters in court, and who didn't think much of the encounter. While doing my own research, I found a footnote in the November 1863 *Proceedings of the Massachusetts Historical Society*, which claims that an acquaintance of Obour Tanner told someone else that Tanner had told her—keep up, now; this is getting complicated—that Tanner did not like Peters, that Wheatley had "let herself down" by marrying him. But this same footnote giving this ostensible inside information also gets Wheatley's death date wrong, by ten years.

Even if Wheatley did, as Odell claims, give birth to children who died in infancy—and at present, there is no documentation for that—infant mortality rates were disturbingly high during this period. It was not uncommon for parents to lose several offspring in infancy or childhood, even those parents who fed, clothed, and loved their children. There would have been nothing for Peters to forestall a child's death from a disease such as measles. As for Wheatley's passing and whether Peters had a direct or indirect hand in it, there is no proof that he pushed her into an early grave, either. In the eighteenth century, life spans were short for whites, and even shorter for African Americans. Wheatley died around the age of thirty-three, which, unfortunately, is in keeping with life expectancies for black women in America at that time.

Carretta supplies evidence that, at the time of Wheatley's death, Peters was living in Massachusetts indeed, but he was in prison because he couldn't pay his bills. (In twenty-first-century terms, he had bad credit.) This is not a crime by our contemporary standards, but it was during Peters's time. There was an economic depression in New England, in the aftermath of the American Revolution; many people in Massachusetts, black and white, couldn't pay their bills or even afford food. Starvation was not unheard of.

Peters was released from jail, and, according to Carretta, for the next sixteen years, he continued to aspire to the role of gentleman. And now we have definitive proof that Peters also kept trying to publish the second book of poetry that his late wife had written. In October 2015, I corresponded (by e-mail) with the assistant curator of manuscripts at the American Antiquarian Society. Knowing my interest in the Wheatley-Peters marriage, she shared with me an excerpt of a never-published letter (dated June 2, 1791) between the printers Ebenezer T. Andrews and Isaiah Thomas. In this letter, Andrews refers to a "proposal" for "Wheatley's Poems," and that he had promised Peters that they would "print them" and split the "neat profits with him." But bewilderingly, that second book never appeared.

Carretta notes that Peters died in 1801; he was fifty-five at the time of his death. He never was able to pay off his debts, but he left some nice belongings behind. A horse, a desk, some leather-bottomed chairs. Books, which meant he not only was literate, but may also have enjoyed reading.

When you look at Peters's life, okay, the brother "did a couple bids," but at least he didn't leave behind any *people* that had to be sold to erase his debts, as Jefferson did. Families were broken up, auctioned off, and sifted like chaff. That would be the fate of the slaves of Monticello after Jefferson died. I can't help but wonder what Odell would have thought of his actions.

I have continued my research on Wheatley. I regularly search for new information; I read new articles about her, and always, I check the notes and the bibliography. Periodically, I look for primary materials to see if any new information on her has emerged. When finances permit, I travel and do my primary research in person.

In the meantime, I publish poems based upon Wheatley research. In 2010, I published an essay on her as well, mentioning my sighting of Peters on that 1790 census, dis-

cussing the unproven connection between Odell and the
Wheatley family:

> [It] is distressing that, in 176 years, scholars have not ques-
> tioned Odell's right to speak for Phillis Wheatley. This blind
> trust continues the disturbing historical trend of African
> Americans, and black women in particular, needing white
> benefactors to justify their lives and history.

The thing is, I have fallen in love with Wheatley and I
want to do right by her legacy. I want to get everything cor-
rect, but if I'm not the one to uncover new information, if
someone else finds it, that isn't a problem for me. I just want
it to be found. I have hoped that by pointing to the absence
of documentation on Odell, researchers will take notice and
renew the search for her genealogy. If no family records
can be identified, then the responsible, professional cause
of action would be to cease using Odell as a primary source
for Wheatley's life. The other option would be to catego-
rize *Memoir* as historical fiction, but whatever the catego-
rization, someone must directly challenge Odell's authority
to provide the most enduring depiction of Wheatley, and of
her husband as a sycophant and a hustler.

I've tried to be pragmatic when it comes to the work of
Wheatley biographers and scholars. Research is hard. It's
time-consuming and frustrating; I know that from personal
experience. Furthermore, there often isn't much information to go on. For example, if Odell's *Memoir* were to be
eliminated as a primary source for Wheatley's life, what else

would be left to rely upon? Precious little. Yes, a chronicle that may not be fully accurate is more than exists for most eighteenth-century, formerly enslaved black folks, but really, these traces provide a pitiful tribute to the woman who is the mother of African American literature.

Never mind that controversial, beginning line of her poem "'Twas mercy brought me from my *Pagan* land . . ." Wheatley is much more than that. She proved something to white people about us: that we could read and think and write—and damn it, we could *feel*, no matter what the racists believed. We already knew those things about ourselves. I'm pretty positive about that, but during her time, philosophers were arranging the "nations" with Africans at the bottom, while other Europeans measured black people's skulls alongside those of orangutans to determine if the two species were kissing cousins. In the midst of these soul assaults, Wheatley's poems carried the weight for African people on this side of the Atlantic. As a result, Wheatley—along with black soldiers and sailors who fought on the winning side of the American Revolution, black intellectuals and writers, and various individuals of African descent asserting their God-given rights of liberty—helped to sway many white Americans and Europeans that slavery was wrong.

Yet I'm waiting for someone to write a more emotionally charged book about Wheatley, one that would take into account her pre-American existence. Although she was a little girl when she arrived in Boston, and although the Wheatleys were "kind" to her, she did have African birth parents. Her life did not begin in America or with slavery. She had a free lineage that did not include the Wheatleys. If nothing else, a treatment of precolonial West African history, along with the eighteenth-century culture of that region, would be an appropriate and respectful introduction to Wheatley's life in America.

In addition, I'm waiting for someone to include a compassionate, well-fleshed depiction of John Peters, which considers how he fit into African American intellectual, commercial, and activist life of the Revolutionary era. Perhaps I seem naïve or silly, but I'd like scholars to view him as a natural occurrence in Wheatley's trajectory, instead of a low-down disruption that led to her demise. Oddly, no account that I've read of Peters gives the most obvious, commonsense reason for why Wheatley might have married him.

Maybe he didn't trick her. She wasn't desperate or temporarily out of her mind. They married because they were deeply, passionately in love.

Is that explanation so ridiculous? Why wouldn't they love each other? American people of African descent did fall in love back then, and, if allowed by local power structures, they legally married. They did this in the midst of war, slavery, economic chaos, and/or posttraumatic stress over being torn from their homelands and sent over the horrific Middle Passage. I think it's logical to assume that many, many black folk fell in love with many, many other black folk. This assumption is a rational consequence of acknowledging black humanity.

At times, when I'm impatiently waiting for scholars to reexamine the complicated realities of these two people,

I imagine Phillis and John, what their moments together might have been.

Maybe Peters thought Wheatley was beautiful. He was drawn to her delicate face, to her very dark skin, her full lips, her tight, kinky hair, to the ring in her nose that might have been an ornament she carried from across the water. (Look very closely at that engraving in her book. Use a magnifying glass and you will see that nose ring.)

And maybe Wheatley thought Peters handsome. He might have looked like her relatives, back in the Gambia that she wrote about. She and Peters might have shared a hankering for a place that lived only in their memories. He might have been born in America—we probably will never know—but in any case, he would have been of African heritage. Maybe at night, when they settled down together in their rickety bed, they talked in whispers, telling each other stories of that faraway place across the water. Folktales or proverbs that had been passed down.

He possessed ambitions, the same as she, and instead of stories, maybe they talked about the future, their hopes for his fledgling businesses and her new book of poetry, the glories that would be accomplished by their children. Anything was possible in that time, when messages of liberty abounded.

Maybe he was a tender lover and they laughed and cried and clutched. The words they spoke after their passion were to be believed, even though they came from the mouths of black folk.

White Rage

CAROL ANDERSON

When we look back on what happened in Ferguson, Missouri, during the summer of 2014, it will be easy to think of it as yet one more episode of black rage ignited by yet another police killing of an unarmed African American male. But that has it precisely backward. What we've actually seen is the latest outbreak of white rage. Sure, it is cloaked in the niceties of law and order, but it is rage nonetheless.

Protests and looting naturally capture attention. But the real rage smolders in meetings where officials redraw precincts to dilute African American voting strength or seek to slash the government payrolls that have long served as sources of black employment. It goes virtually unnoticed, however, because white rage doesn't have to take to the streets and face rubber bullets to be heard. Instead, white rage carries an aura of respectability and has access to the courts, police, legislatures, and governors, who cast its efforts as noble, though they are actually driven by the most ignoble motivations.

White rage recurs in American history. It exploded after the Civil War, erupted again to undermine the Supreme Court's *Brown v. Board of Education* decision, and took on its latest incarnation with Barack Obama's ascent to the White House. For every action of African American advancement, there's a reaction, a backlash.

The North's victory in the Civil War did not bring peace. Instead, emancipation brought white resentment that the good ol' days of black subjugation were over. Legislatures throughout the South scrambled to reinscribe white supremacy and restore the aura of legitimacy that the antislavery campaign had tarnished. Lawmakers in several states created the Black Codes, which effectively criminalized blackness, sanctioned forced labor, and undermined every tenet of democracy. Even the federal authorities' promise of 40 acres—land seized from traitors who had tried to destroy the United States of America—crumbled like dust.

Influential white legislators such as Rep. Thaddeus Stevens (R-Pa.) and Sen. Charles Sumner (R-Mass.) tried to make this nation live its creed, but they were no match for the swelling resentment that neutralized the Thirteenth, Fourteenth, and Fifteenth amendments, and welcomed the Supreme Court's 1876 *United States v. Cruikshank* decision, which undercut a law aimed at stopping the terror of the Ku Klux Klan.

Nearly eighty years later, *Brown v. Board of Education* seemed like another moment of triumph—with the ruling on the unconstitutionality of separate public schools for black and white students affirming African Americans' rights as citizens. But black children, hungry for quality education, ran headlong into more white rage. Bricks and mobs at school doors were only the most obvious signs. In

March 1956, 101 members of Congress issued the Southern Manifesto, declaring war on the *Brown* decision. Governors in Virginia, Arkansas, Alabama, Georgia, and elsewhere then launched "massive resistance." They created a legal doctrine, interposition, that supposedly nullified any federal law or court decision with which a state disagreed. They passed legislation to withhold public funding from any school that abided by *Brown*. They shut down public school systems and used tax dollars to ensure that whites could continue their education at racially exclusive private academies. Black children were left to rot with no viable option.

A little more than half a century after *Brown*, the election of Obama gave hope to the country and the world that a new racial climate had emerged in America, or that it would. But such audacious hopes would be short-lived. A rash of voter-suppression legislation, a series of unfathomable Supreme Court decisions, the rise of stand-your-ground laws, and continuing police brutality make clear that Obama's election and reelection have unleashed yet another wave of fear and anger.

It's more subtle—less overtly racist—than in 1865 or even 1954. It's a remake of the Southern Strategy, crafted in the wake of the civil rights movement to exploit white resentment against African Americans, and deployed with precision by Presidents Richard Nixon and Ronald Reagan. As Reagan's key political strategist, Lee Atwater, explained in a 1981 interview: "You start out in 1954 by saying, 'N— —-, n— —-, n— —-.' By 1968 you can't say 'n— —-'—that hurts you. Backfires. So you say stuff like 'forced busing,' 'states' rights,' and all that stuff. You're getting so abstract now you're talking about cutting taxes, and all these things you're talking about are totally economic things, and a byproduct of them is blacks get hurt worse than whites. And subconsciously maybe that is part of it. I'm not saying that." (The interview was originally published anonymously, and only years later did it emerge that Atwater was the subject.)

Now, under the guise of protecting the sanctity of the ballot box, conservatives have devised measures—such as photo ID requirements—to block African Americans' access to the polls. A joint report by the NAACP Legal Defense and Educational Fund and the NAACP emphasized that the ID requirements would adversely affect more than 6 million African American voters. (Twenty-five percent of black Americans lack a government-issued photo ID, the report noted, compared with only 8 percent of white Americans.) The Supreme Court sanctioned this discrimination in *Shelby County v. Holder*, which gutted the Voting Rights Act and opened the door to twenty-first-century versions of nineteenth-century literacy tests and poll taxes.

The economic devastation of the Great Recession also shows African Americans under siege. The foreclosure crisis hit black Americans harder than any other group in the United States. A 2013 report by researchers at Brandeis University calculated that "half the collective wealth of African-American families was stripped away during the Great Recession," in large part because of the impact on home equity. In the process, the wealth gap between blacks and whites grew: Right before the recession, white Americans had four times more wealth than black Americans, on average; by 2010, the gap had increased to six times. This was a targeted hit. Communities of color were far more likely to have riskier, higher-interest-rate loans than white communities, with good credit scores often making no difference.

Add to this the tea party movement's assault on so-called Big Government, which despite the sanitized language of fiscal responsibility constitutes an attack on African American jobs. Public-sector employment, where there is less discrimination in hiring and pay, has traditionally been an important venue for creating a black middle class.

So when you think of Ferguson, don't just think of black resentment at a criminal justice system that allows a white police officer to put six bullets into an unarmed black teen. Consider the economic dislocation of black America. Remember a Florida judge instructing a jury to focus only on the moment when George Zimmerman and Trayvon Martin interacted, thus transforming a seventeen-year-old, unarmed kid into a big, scary black guy, while the grown man who stalked him through the neighborhood with a loaded gun becomes a victim. Remember the assault on the Voting Rights Act. Look at *Connick v. Thompson*, a partisan 5–4 Supreme Court decision in 2011 that ruled it was legal for a city prosecutor's staff to hide evidence that exonerated a black man who was rotting on death row for fourteen years. And think of a recent study by Stanford University psychology researchers concluding that when white people were told that black Americans are incarcerated in numbers far beyond their proportion of the population "they reported being more afraid of crime and more likely to support the kinds of punitive policies that exacerbate the racial disparities," such as three-strikes or stop-and-frisk laws.

Only then does Ferguson make sense. It's about white rage.

Cracking the Code

JESMYN WARD

When my father moved to Oakland, California, after Hurricane Camille wrecked the Mississippi Gulf Coast, in 1969, strangers he encountered from El Salvador and Mexico and Puerto Rico would spit rapid-fire Spanish at him, expecting a reply in kind. "Are you Samoan?" a Samoan asked him once. But my father, with his black, silky hair that curled into Coke-bottle waves at the ends, skin the color of milky tea, and cheekbones like dorsal fins breaking the water of his face, was none of these things. He attended an all-black high school in Oakland; in his class pictures, his is one of the few light faces. His hair is parted in the middle and falls away in a blowsy afro, coarsened to the right texture by multiple applications of relaxer.

My father was born in 1956 in Pass Christian, a small Mississippi town on the coast of the Gulf of Mexico, fifty miles from New Orleans. He grew up in a dilapidated single-story house: four rooms, with a kitchen tacked onto the back. It was built along the railroad tracks and shook when trains sped by; the wood of the sloped floor rotted at the corners. The house was nothing like the great columned mansions strung along the man-made beach just half a mile or so down the road, houses graced with front-facing balconies so that the wealthy white families who lived in them could gaze out at the flat pan of the water and the searing, pale sand, where mangrove trees had grown before they'd bulldozed the land.

Put simply, my father grew up as a black boy in a black family in the deep South, where being black, in the sixties, was complicated. The same was true in the eighties, when I was growing up in DeLisle, a town a few miles north of Pass Christian. Once, when I was a teen, we stood together in a drugstore checkout line behind an older, blondish white woman. My father, an inveterate joker, kept shoving me between my shoulder blades, trying to make me stumble into her. "Daddy, stop," I mouthed, as I tried to avoid a collision. I was horrified: Daddy's going to make me knock this white woman over. Then she turned around, and I realized that it was my grandaunt Eunice, my grandmother's sister—that she was blood. "I thought you were white," I said, and she and my father laughed.

Coastal Mississippi is a place where Eunice—a woman pale as milk, with blond hair and African heritage—is considered, and considers herself, black. The one-drop rule is real here. Eunice wasn't allowed on the beaches of the Gulf Coast or Lake Pontchartrain until the early seventies. The state so fiercely neglected her education that her grandfather established a community school for black children. Once Eunice graduated, after the eighth grade, her schooling was done. She worked in her father's fields, and then as a cleaning woman for the white families in their mansions on the coast. On the local TV station, she watched commentators discuss what it meant to be a proper Creole, women who were darker than her asserting that true Creoles have only Spanish and French ancestry. Theirs was part of an ongoing attempt to write anyone with African or Native American heritage out of the region's history; to erase us from the story of the plantations, the swamps, the bayou; to deny that plaçage, those unofficial unions, during the time of antimiscegenation laws, between European men and women of African heritage had ever taken place.

It's impossible for most black Americans to construct full family trees. Official census records, used by so many genealogy enthusiasts to piece together their families' pasts, don't include our non-European ancestors. Both my mother's and my father's family name is Dedeaux (I bear my paternal grandmother's last name), and several relatives on my mother's side have traced their lineage through European Dedeauxs back to France, but building a family tree of people of color is far harder. I always understood my ancestry, like that of so many others on the Gulf Coast, to be a tangle of African slaves, free men of color, French and Spanish immigrants, British colonists, Native Americans— but in what proportion, and what might that proportion tell me about who I thought I was?

I was at a dinner with some professors from Spring Hill College in Mobile, Alabama, when one of them told me about the genetic-testing company 23andMe. It cost ninety-nine dollars—that was my first surprise. I imagined that the price of such a service would be exorbitant, but evidently it wasn't. You order a kit online, the professor explained, and get it in the mail a week or so later, then register it on the company's website, spit into a test tube, seal it, and send it back in the provided box. Around six weeks later, you receive your results. The professor said that his girlfriend had spent hours poring over hers, fascinated by her genetically based health analysis. (Due to an FDA crackdown, 23andMe no longer provides that particular service.) But I was interested in genetic testing for a different reason.

I ordered tests for my father, my mother, and myself. We submitted our samples, then waited for the company's scientists to decode the ancestral information in our DNA.

My mother and I were sitting at her kitchen table when her test came back. My father was at my sister's house, surrounded by his children, when he received his. Their results confirmed some of the notions we'd had about our ancestry, as passed down through family lore, and subverted others. My father, who'd always believed himself to have Native American heritage, and who had a strong affinity for Native American history and culture, found that he is 51 percent Native American, as well as nearly equal parts sub-Saharan African and European (British, Irish, Spanish, and Ashkenazi)—23.5 percent and 22.5 percent, respectively—and just over 1 percent North African. My mother, who has told me story after story about her white great-grandparents taking their mixed-race children to visit their families in Kiln, Mississippi, only to hide the kids in the trunk of the car at the end of every visit when the sun set and it was no longer safe, found that she is 55 percent European—a mixture of British, Irish, French, German, Scandinavian, and Iberian—41 percent sub-Saharan African, and 3.4 percent Native American.

My parents' results gave them the concrete proof of their ancestry that they'd always been denied. My father, a former member of the Black Panther party, proudly claimed his Native American heritage by registering with the Choctaw tribe of Slidell, Louisiana. My mother could at last make educated guesses about the parentage of her great-grandparents. It was as if 23andMe had taught them to read the language of their family histories, enabling them to finally understand the incomprehensible book of their ancestral pasts: to read what had been gibberish.

Yet I found my own results both surprising and troubling. I was raised in Mississippi, in a family and a community that identified as black, and I have the stories and the experiences to go with it. One of my great-great-grandfathers was killed by a gang of white Prohibition patrollers. My mother helped to integrate the local elementary school in the 1960s. My father was run out of segregated Pass Christian's beaches and the local park. I was the only black girl at my private high school in Pass Christian, the target of my classmates' backward ideas about race. Despite my parents' sense of their mixed roots, I had thought that my genetic makeup would confirm the identity that I'd grown up with—one that located Africa as my ancestors' primary point of origin, and that allowed me to claim a legacy of black resistance and strength.

So it was discomfiting to find that my ancestry was 40

percent European—a mixture of British, Irish, French, German, Scandinavian, Iberian, Italian, and Ashkenazi—32 percent sub-Saharan African, a quarter Native American, and less than 1 percent North African. For a few days after I received my results, I looked into the mirror and didn't know how to understand myself. I tried to understand my heritage through my features, to assign each one a place, but I couldn't. All I could see was my hair: hair that grows up and out instead of falling flat, like my father's; hair that refuses to be as smooth and tidy as my mother's but instead bushes and tangles and curls in all directions at once. Mine is a mane that bears the strongest imprint of my African ancestors, hair that my stylist combed out into a voluminous afro during one of my visits to New York City, so that I walked the streets with a ten-inch halo that repelled the rain and spoke of Africa to everyone who saw it.

That's how I remembered myself. I remembered that people of color from my region of the United States can choose to embrace all aspects of their ancestry, in the food they eat, in the music they listen to, in the stories they tell, while also choosing to war in one armor, that of black Americans, when they fight for racial equality. I remembered that in choosing to identify as black, to write about black characters in my fiction and to assert the humanity of black people in my nonfiction, I've remained true to my personal history, to my family history, to my political and moral choices, and to my essential self: a self that understands the world through the prism of being a black American, and stands in solidarity with the people of the African diaspora.

This doesn't mean that I don't honor and claim the myriad other aspects of my heritage. I do, in ways serious and silly. I read Philip Larkin and Seamus Heaney and love all things Harry Potter and *Doctor Who*. I study French and Spanish and attempt to translate the simplest poems by Pablo Neruda and Federico García Lorca into English (and fail awfully). I watch obscure French movies with subtitles. I attend powwows and eat fry bread and walk along the outside of the dancing circles with a kind of wistful longing because I want to understand the singing so badly, because I want to stomp the earth in exultation and to belong in that circle, too. But I imagine that my ancestors from Sierra Leone and Britain, from France and the Choctaw settlements on the Mississippi bayou, from Spain and Ghana—all those people whose genetic strands intertwined to produce mine—felt that same longing, even as they found themselves making a new community here at the mouth of the Mississippi. Together, they would make new music, like blues and jazz and zydeco, and new dances, second lining through the streets. They would make a world that reflected back to them the richness of their heritage, and in doing so discover a new type of belonging.

PART II

RECKONING

Queries of Unrest

CLINT SMITH

After Hanif Willis-Abdurraqib

Maybe I come from the gap
between my father's teeth.
Maybe I was meant to see a little
bit of darkness every time he smiled.

Maybe I was meant to understand that
darkness magnifies the sight of joy.
Maybe I come from where the sidewalk
ends, or maybe I just read that in a book once.
It can be hard to tell the difference sometimes.

Maybe that's because when I was a kid
a white boy told me I was marginalized
and all I could think of was the edge
of a sheet of paper, how empty it is—
the abyss I was told never to write into.

Maybe I'm scared of writing another poem
that makes people roll their eyes

and say, "another black poem."
Maybe I'm scared people won't think
of the poem as a poem, but as a cry for help.

Maybe the poem is a cry for help.

Maybe I come from a place where people
are always afraid of dying.
Maybe that's just what I tell myself
so I don't feel so alone in this body.
Maybe there's a place where everyone is both
in love with and running from their own skin.
Maybe that place is here.

Maybe that's why I'm always running from
the things that love me. Maybe I'm trying
to save them the time of burying darkness
when all they have to do is close their eyes.

Blacker Than Thou

KEVIN YOUNG

It was never easy for me. I was born a poor black child . . .

The beginning of Steve Martin's *The Jerk* still makes me laugh with its twist on Once Upon a Time. The dissonance between what we know of the white comedian Martin, his relative success, and his obviously false declaration sends up not only the tragic showbiz biography but the corny black one: in both, the worser, the better. It also suggests his character's transformation, his overcoming—after all, he's clearly white now!—not to mention his current lot in which he's as smudged, bummy, apparently destitute. His isn't blackface, but his face half-greased is certainly part of the effect—it's a familiar one, in other words, to black people used to watching white people only claim blackness as a "poor me" stance.

Now, why does this jerk remind me of Rachel Dolezal?

There's a long-standing American tradition of whites donning blackface, or redface, or any other colored mask they pretend is a face. Those who wear blackface reduce blackness to skin in order not to be white. The implication of course is that black people are just miscolored or extra-dark white people. Many a joke told for my benefit in my Kansas grade school reinforced the same. *Know why black people's palms are white?*

But if you are white but truly "feel black" then why do you have to look like it?

My next nonfiction book, *Unoriginal Sin*, is about hoaxers and impostors, plagiarists and phonies. I finished it last week and sent it in to my publisher, elated and relieved. Now I have to take time to write about Rachel Dolezal too?

I can't decide if Dolezal, the woman revealed to have been merely pretending to be black, lecturing as such and even leading her local Oregon NAACP, is the natural extension of what I've been saying in my next book, or a distraction from this larger point: that quite regularly, faced with the paradox of race, the hoax rears its head. It turns out, I now know, it rears its rear too.

When Rachel Dolezal first broke, and was simply a joke on Black Twitter, I identified some of my favorite Twitter titles for the inevitable, anticipated memoir: "Their Eyes Were Watching Oprah" (that one's mine); "Imitation of Imitation of Life" (from Victor LaValle); "Blackish Like Me" (mine too). Now things done got serious.

When you are black, you don't have to look like it, but you do have to look at it. Or look around. Blackness is the face in the mirror, a not-bad-looking one, that for no reason at all some people uglify or hate on or wish ill for, to, about. Sometimes any lusting after it gets to be a drag too.

Every black person has something "not black" about them. I don't mean something white, because despite our easy dichotomies, the opposite of black is not white. This one likes European classical music; that one likes a little bit of country (hopefully the old stuff); this one is the first African American principal ballerina; this one can't dance. Black people know this—any solidarity with each other is about something shared, a secret joy, a song, not about some stereotypical qualities that may be reproducible, imitable, even marketable. This doesn't mean there aren't similarities across black people or communities or better yet memory—just that these aren't exactly about bodies and not really about skin at all, but culture.

There is a long tradition of passing—of racial crossing the line, usually going from black to white. You could say it was started, like this country, by Thomas Jefferson.

• • •

One of the best things about being black is that, barring some key exceptions, it's not a volunteer position. You can't just wish on a dark star and become black. It's not paid either. It's more like a long internship with a chance of advancement.

I've never seen the TV show *Blackish* all the way through. (I hear it's quite good now.) From what I've seen, *Fresh Off the Boat*, another of ABC's offerings, seems to me a more accurate portrayal of the complexity of racial identity, even black identity. (This is despite the worries of its creator, chef and author Eddie Huang.) The young Asian immigrant who's the main character identifies with hip-hop in order to be both American and remain and help explain being *nonwhite*. It's funny, and frequently brilliant: How *do* you become American?

Is this the same as becoming black?

Traditionally, pretend blackness was the fastest route to becoming white. This is true for Irish and Jewish immigrants, who adopted blackface in large numbers in the late nineteenth and early twentieth, and soon assimilated; and for Northerners, for whom blackface helped them imagine themselves a nation since blackface's advent in the 1830s.

Cue that f'in caricature of Jim Crow dancing.

• • •

Like Rachel Dolezal, I too became black around the age of five. I first became a nigger at nine, so I had me a good run.

The problem isn't just that Rachel Dolezal can wash off whatever she's sprayed on herself (it just don't look right), or that blackness is a choice, but that what she's wearing isn't just bronzer, but *blacker*: a notion that blackness is itself hyperbolic, excessive, skin tone only. Well, and wigs.

This last, some black observers have praised.

Did Dolezal really fool those black folks around her? I have a strange feeling she didn't, that many simply humored her. You have to do this with white people, from time to time.

Black people are constantly identifying and recognizing those who look like secret black folks—many light-skinned people I know get identified as white by white people, but we know they're black. (This isn't passing, btw.) Most look like one of my aunties. Knowing they are black, it is hard to see them another way.

It's one of the advantages of my folks being from Louisiana—there's lots of folks who don't "look black" but are (which of course should make us stop and reevaluate what "looking black" is). Because of the one-drop rule, though begun as a controlling race law, black people themselves adapted and even invented and accepted a broader blackness. In general this has made black people—I am speaking for every single black person without exception here, of course—wary yet accepting.

Those surprised by a white lady darkening her skin and curling her hair haven't been out of the house or online in a while.

There was the rather white-looking bank manager in Athens, Georgia, who chatted me up one day and mentioned a couple key black striver things—a black sorority here, the Links there—that let me know she was black too. It was brilliant, and in no way calculated; hers was smart survival.

It was also a test to see if I was woke, or a striver, too.

Teaching a class about blackness doesn't mean you are black. Blackness isn't a bunch of facts to memorize, or a set of stock behaviors; nor darker skin color neither. It's like the jazz heads I've seen, often white, who can tell you every sideman on every session, but seem in the daylight unable to find the beat. The beat is there always; doesn't mean you can always hear it.

While black folks often hear the beat, and set it, doesn't mean when anyone else hears it, that she gets to be black.

Every church I know of had a white lady who arrived one day. Ours in Topeka did. After she hung around awhile, and proved herself she wasn't a tourist, "Mrs. Pete" was accepted and seen as part of the AME congregation, even singing in the choir (which was a high bar, as it were). But we never thought she was, or somehow became, black. *She's good people*, folks would say.

She did get herself a perm: I mean a white, curly one, instead of a straightened, black one; a clarification that's one more sign we're awfully mixed up. There's the joke: *You didn't get yourself a perm, but a temporary.*

There is the other, far rarer passing, which we may call reverse-passing, of whites living as black. The most prominent I know of may be Johnny Otis—who was successful enough that many race women and men I know aren't aware he was actually born white. Or the Baseball Hall of Fame inductee, owner of a Negro League team who likely wasn't black herself. What's interesting is to wonder what the black people around them thought, usually accepting them—not necessarily as what they said they were, but how they acted. It isn't that they weren't judged, just that when they were, they weren't found wanting.

• • •

So when the killer [name withheld] walked into Mother Emanuel Church in Charleston one week after the Dolezal story broke, I am not surprised that the black worshippers there welcomed him. Welcome is an integral part of the African American Christian tradition; it is especially so in the African Methodist Episcopal one, begun over two hundred years ago when the Methodist church prevented blacks, mostly freedmen and women, to pray beside its whites, even pulling them off their knees.

How long did [name redacted] sit there waiting, deciding to deny the evidence of humanity before him? Nothing, it appears, could have convinced him not to kill blacks, whom he believed—and spewed hate about—preyed on white people, especially women. One suspects he may not've known any women besides his family.

Thomas Jefferson hated black people but slept with one who bore his children, six of them. (*Misery is often the parent of the most affecting touches in poetry.—Among the blacks is misery enough, God knows, but no poetry*, he wrote in *Notes on Virginia*.) That Sally Hemings was also his wife's half-sister neither stopped him nor did it make him reevaluate his stance toward black thought, which he saw as an impossible paradox.

Jefferson had black heirs who he, and for centuries his (sorta) white heirs and white defenders, denied. In our time,

Strom Thurmond had him a black daughter out of wedlock; the only people surprised by this were the white voters he courted by vehement racist rhetoric. Of course, this behavior, demeaning blacks while desiring at least one, descends from slavery and is how we got most light-skinned folks who "look white" in the first place.

Why doesn't Rachel Dolezal seem to know that a white person can have a black child (see one-drop rule above)? (See Obama.) (See Hemings.) (See Jefferson.) See . . .

Being black is not a feeling. *I don't always feel colored.* Nor is it simply a state of mind.

Blackness: a way of being.

It would be one thing, I think, if in her house, to her pillow or family, Dolezal said she felt black. I imagine many white households across the country don blackface and grab banjos and have themselves a good ol' time when no one else is around. It's when that somehow translates to what she does, when she teaches black studies as if she's a black person—not a teacher, but a mind reader—that it becomes a problem. She wears the mask not to hide but to gain authority over the very thing she claims to want to be. How very white of her!

After Rachel Dolezal had mumbled her way through various news shows looking like Gilly from *Saturday Night Live* and answered the question of whether she was black or not with *I don't understand the question*, came the murders in cold blood at Mother Emanuel Church in Charleston. Both cases didn't seem just coincidental, but near-simultaneous misapprehensions not just of blackness but of whiteness too.

After the killings in Charleston, several things happened: Dolezal's story went back to merely being ridiculous. Talk shows moved on to something else and those who somehow willed Dolezal sublime retreated. Flags flew at half staff—except the Confederate flag on South Carolina statehouse grounds. It took a black woman to climb up and take that down.

They gave the assignment to a black man to raise the "rebel flag," the stars and bars, back up. Like Sally Hemings, he might not have minded, but he certainly couldn't have refused.

Soon the Confederate battle flag would be voted down by the state assembly, but flag sales would soar. Customers began to hoard them like guns once most major outlets suspended sales. Yet given the killer's postings of himself with Confederate flags and separatist slogans, easy slogans like "heritage not hate" stood naked. The proof here only increased as a pro-flag rally brought out the American Nazi flag, side by side and even mashed up with the Confederate one.

In a place like the South that loves its tall tales, why do people take their Confederate stories hyperseriously? As gospel? *Everyone's a colonel*, someone joked with me about the South when I was at the University of Georgia, where I taught for five years.

It was my first job, and I was regularly thought by strangers at the university to be passing for a student (and not a grad student). *You look too young to be a professor*, surprised interrogators would say, usually after asking what year in school I was. (It's true I was only twenty-five, but had a book already and a degree or two.) After a while, I began to translate the comment about looking young to be a more polite way of saying what they couldn't: *You look too black to be a professor.*

Maybe blackness is only a look, one we're told cannot ever look back?

Far more interesting and provocative than a white mother in blackface would be a white mother with black children. Wouldn't that provide a much more complex identity than any blackface? You get the feeling that, for Dolezal, blackness equals hiding.

For the deaconess at the church who had to make her way by cleaning white people's houses during the week, black-

111

ness don't mean hiding. Sunday meant rest, and a respite, wearing a different kind of white, black hair crowned by lace.

Blackness too often veers between two poles in the public eye: opaqueness and invisibility. For [racist killer], blackness wasn't just opaque but conspicuous. It named an enemy and provided a uniform that allowed mass judgment—and murder.

Rachel Dolezal could be conspicuously outraged all the time, filing lawsuits, marching, because she didn't have to save any energy for just being herself.

Dolezal's drama didn't just start recently. The persecution complex, the past lawsuits (when she was white) against a historically black institution like Howard University no less, seem like the whitest thing ever. It's like when you are with a white friend and they experience racism, likely for the first time, alongside you: they usually go wild, protesting no one and everyone; you shrug as much as shout. Some things are just part of the daily dose of being black. The cab will drive away with a white friend in it rather than drive you too. It's dealing with blackness that black people have perfected—or at least gotten practiced at.

Racism's daily injustices are almost an inoculation against it. Almost.

• • •

Whenever I tell a white person about the injustices at the airport, or on the street, the daily snubs, or that my white neighbor's farewell to me as I was moving out of my apartment last year was *Goodbye, nigger* and that no one in the condos or its board, both painted white, did a thing about it, they too grow silent.

Part of grief, I've found, is silence. Protest too, at times. What the no-longer-neighbor wanted from me most, I knew instantly, was a reaction. *Bye*, I said. Good riddance, I meant.

I've heard even Dolezal's paintings of black faces while in school as a white graduate student at Howard were actually plagiarized. Our Dolezal didn't just want to disappear into blackness, but disappear. For her, blackness was not a private thing, which ultimately may be where blackness best tells us what it knows. It is this private, shifting, personal blackness that cannot be borrowed. What can be: wigs, tanning booth, rhetoric.

Dolezal's righteous rage looks more like self-righteousness — or is it other-righteousness?

What no one seems to say is just how Dolezal's actions, over many years, conform to the typical hoaxer's: a constant shifting set of stories to explain her identity (it's complicated), an array of attempts to be not just someone else as anyone might, but to be exotic, even in her birth (which she said was in a teepee or tipi). When asked directly on the teevee if she was born in a teepee, she answered, "I wasn't born *in* a teepee," emphasis allowing that maybe, just maybe, she could later say she was born near or under one. The hoaxer is always leaving the pretend teepee door ajar.

Dolezal also says she was abused, and claimed to have lived in South Africa. It is true that her actual parents did live there, but not with her, only her siblings—many of whom were actually adopted and black. She apparently earlier equated their alleged beatings (that several of them have denied) with slavery. Given her disproven lies, abuse does not so much provide an explanation for her behavior as much as a distraction: true or not, like her making slavery a mere metaphor it would seem part of a scenario of victimhood, which to her is also, inherently, black.

Borrowed blackness and nativeness provide her the ultimate virtual victimhood.

Finally the chief problem with racial impostors or blackface: it can be only, as James Weldon Johnson said of stereotypical black dialect, comic or tragic. Ultimately, it conforms to white views of "the blacks" themselves, off-stage: as either a joke or a set of jailed youths and stooped old people.

Even the president, who started up a Twitter feed weeks before the Dolezal incident, was inundated by racists posting pictures of nooses and equating him to a monkey or worse. It is only when one feels such stereotypes as real that one might find being in blackface freeing—not because you believe the stereotypes, but because you want to establish other, corny ones.

Sinking feeling: blackfaced person always occupies a bigger public stage than a black one.

Standing back, maybe it's true: not that being black is only comic or tragic, but that too often white thinking or acting out about it, as demonstrated in Dolezal's hoax and the Charleston murders, remains only polarized: comic or tragic. Both are nullifying.

Amid the bewilderment and grief, for just a moment I wondered how onetime NAACP chapter leader Dolezal would've responded, as surely she would have sought to, had she not been unmasked. Where's our fearless leader now? I thought. Then I didn't think of her again.

I came out as black as a teenager. Before then, I was simply a boy. After, I was sometimes, still.

• • •

When President Obama broke into "Amazing Grace" at the funeral for those killed at Mother Emanuel, it was mere hours after the Supreme Court declared gay marriage legal, and barring it as unconstitutional. There it was strange yet strangely fitting to hear him sing that song written by the reformed slaver while at sea. I like to think the slaves who took the song over and made it a Negro spiritual were not the same kinds of *wretch* as its author.

Of course you can see why anyone would want to be black: being black is fun. Don't tell nobody.

This morning I woke from a "deep Negro sleep," as Senghor put it. I then took a black shower and shaved a black shave; I walked a black walk and sat a black sit; I wrote some black lines; I coughed black and sneezed black and ate black too. This last at least is literal: grapes, blackberries, the ripest plums.

Summer 2015

Da Art of Storytellin' (a Prequel)

KIESE LAYMON

From six in the morning until five in the afternoon, five days a week, for thirty years, my grandmama Catherine's fingers, palms, and wrists wandered deep in the bellies of dead chickens. Grandmama was a buttonhole slicer at a chicken plant in central Mississippi—her job was to slice the belly and pull out the guts of thousands of chickens a day. Grandmama got up every morning around 4:30 a.m. She took her bath, then prepared grits, smoked sausage, and pear preserves for us. After breakfast, Grandmama made me take a teaspoon of cod liver oil "for my vitamins," then she coated the area between her breasts in powder before putting on the clothes she had ironed the night before. I was ten, staying with Grandmama for the summer, and I remember marveling at her preparations and wondering why she got so fresh, so clean, just to leave the house and get dirty.

"There's layers to this," Grandmama often said, when describing her job to folks. She went into that plant every day, knowing it was a laboratory for racial and gendered terror. Still, she wanted to be the best at what she did—and not just the best buttonhole slicer in the plant, but the best, most stylized, most efficient worker in Mississippi.

She understood that the audience for her work was not just her coworkers or her white male shift managers, but all the Southern black women workers who preceded her and, most important, all the Southern black women workers coming next.

By the end of the day, when the two-tone blue Impala crept back into the driveway on the side of our shotgun house, I'd run out to welcome Grandmama home. "Hey, baby," she'd say. "Let me wash this stank off my hands before I hug your neck."

This stank wasn't *that stink*. This stank was root and residue of black Southern poverty, and devalued black Southern labor, black Southern excellence, black Southern imagination, and black Southern woman magic. This was the stank from whence black Southern life, love, and labor came. Even at ten years old, I understood that the presence and necessity of this stank dictated how Grandmama moved on Sundays. As the head of the usher board at Concord Baptist, she sometimes wore the all-white polyester uniform that all the other church ushers wore. On those Sundays, Grandmama was committed to out-freshing the other ushers by draping colorful pearls and fake gold around her neck, or stunting with some shiny shoes she'd gotten from my aunt Linda in Vegas. And Grandmama's outfits, when she wasn't wearing the stale usher board uniform, always had to be fresher this week than the week before.

She was committed to out-freshing herself, which meant that she was up late on Saturday nights, working like a wizard, taking pieces of this blouse from 1984 and sewing them into these dresses from 1969. Grandmama's primary audience on Sundays, her church sisters, looked with awe and envy at her outfits, inferring she had a fashion industry hookup from Atlanta, or a few secret revenue streams. Not so. This was just how Grandmama brought the stank of her work life into her spiritual communal life, in a way that I loved and laughed at as a kid.

I didn't fully understand or feel inspired by Grandmama's stank or freshness until years later, when I heard the albums *ATLiens* and *Aquemini* from those Georgia-based artists called OutKast.

One day near the beginning of my junior year in college, 1996, I walked out of my dorm room in Oberlin, Ohio, heading to the gym, when I heard a new sound and a familiar voice blasting from the room of my friend John Norris, a Southern black boy from Clarksville, Tennessee.

My soliloquy may be hard for some to
    swallow
But so is cod liver oil.

I went into John's room, wondering who was rapping about cod liver oil over reverbed bass, and asked him, "What the fuck is that?" It was "Wheelz of Steel," from *ATLiens*. John handed me the CD. The illustrated cover looked like a comic book, its heroes standing back-to-back in front of a mysterious four-armed force: Big Boi in a letterman jacket with a Braves hat cocked to the right, and André in a green turban like something I'd only seen my Grandmama and Mama Lara rock. Big Boi's fingers were clinched, ready to fight. André's were spread, ready to conjure.

John and I listened to the record twice before I borrowed my friend's green Geo, drove to Elyria, and bought *ATLiens* for myself. Like *Soul Food* by Atlanta's Goodie Mob, another album I was wearing out at the time—their song "Thought Process," which featured André, had nudged me through the sadness of missing Mississippi a year earlier—*ATLiens* was unafraid of the revelatory dimensions of black Southern life. Like *Soul Food*, *ATLliens* explored the inevitability of death and the possibility of new life, new movement, and new mojo.

But something was different.

I already knew OutKast; I loved their first album, *Southernplayalisticadillacmuzik*, in part because of the clever way they interpolated funk and soul into rap. *ATLiens*, however, sounded unlike anything I'd ever heard or imagined. The vocal tones were familiar, but the rhyme patterns, the composition, the production were equal parts red clay, thick buttery grits, and Mars. Nothing sounded like *ATLiens*. The album instantly changed not just my expectations of music, but my expectations of myself as a young black Southern artist.

By then, I already knew I was going to be a writer. I had no idea if I would eat off of what I wrote, but I knew I had to write to be a decent human being. I used ink and the page to probe and to remember through essays and sometimes through satire. I was imitating, and maybe interrogating, but I'm not sure that I had any idea of how to use words to imagine and really innovate. All my English teachers talked about the importance of finding "your voice." It always confused me because I knew we all had so many voices, so many audiences, and my teachers seemed only to really want the kind of voice that sat with its legs crossed, reading *The New York Times.* I didn't have to work to find that cross-legged voice—it was the one education necessitated I lead with.

What my English teachers didn't say was that voices aren't discovered fully formed, they are built and shaped—and not just by words, punctuation, and sentences, but by the author's intended audience, by the composition's form, and by subject. It was only after listening to *ATLiens* that I realized in order to get where I needed to go as a human being and an artist, in order to release my own spacey stank blues, I had to write fiction. Dre and Big showed me it was possible to create fake worlds wholly concerned with "what if" and "maybe" and "what really was."

I remember sitting in my tiny dorm room under my huge Black Lightning poster, next to my tiny picture of Grandmama. I was supposed to be doing a paper on "The Cask of Amontillado," but I was thinking about OutKast's "Wailin'." The song made me know that there was something to be gained, felt, and used in imitating sounds from whence we came, particularly in the minimal hook: the repeated moan of one about to wail. I'd heard that moan in the presence of older Southern black folk my entire life, but I'd never heard it connecting two rhymed verses. Art couldn't get any fresher than that.

By the mid-nineties, hip-hop was an established art form, foregrounding a wide, historically neglected audience in completely new ways. Never had songs had so many words. Never had songs lacked melodies. Never had songs pushed against the notion of a hook repeated every 45 seconds. Like a lot of Southern black boys, I loved New York hip-hop, although I didn't feel loved or imagined by most of it.

When André said, "The South got something to say and that's all I got to say," at the Source awards in 1995, I heard him saying that we were no longer going to artistically follow New York. Not because the artists of New York were wack, but because disregarding our particular stank in favor of a stink that didn't love or respect us was like taking a broken elevator down into artistic and spiritual death.

With OutKast, Dre and Big each carved out their own individual space, and along with sonic contrast—Big lyrically fought and André lyrically conjured—they gave us philosophical contrast. When Dre raps, "No drugs or alcohol so I can get the signal clear as day," I remember folks suggesting there was a smidgen of shade being thrown on Big Boi, who on the same album rhymed, "I got an ounce of dank and a couple of dranks, so let's crank up this session." If there was ever shade between them back then, I got the sense, they'd handle it like we Southern black boys did:

they'd wrassle it out, talk more shit, hug, and come back ready to out-fresh each other, along with every artist who'd come before them in the making of lyrical art.

OutKast created a different kind of stank, too: an urban Southern stank so familiar with and indebted to the gospel, blues, jazz, rock, and funk born in the rural black South. And while they were lyrically competing against each other on track after track, together Big and Dre were united, railing and wailing against New York and standing up to a post-civil-rights South chiding young Southern black boys to pull up our pants and fight white supremacy with swords of respectability and narrow conceptions of excellence. *ATLiens* made me love being black, Southern, celibate, sexy, awkward, free of drugs and alcohol, Grandmama's grandbaby, and cooler than a polar bear's toenails.

Right out of Oberlin, I earned a fellowship in the MFA program at Indiana University, to study fiction. For the first time in my life, I was thinking critically about narrative construction in everything from malt liquor commercials to the Bible. It was around that time that Lauryn Hill gave my generation an elixir to calm, compete with, and call out a culture insistent on coming up with new ways to devalue black women. In *The Miseducation of Lauryn Hill*, I saw myself as the intimate partner doing wrong by Lauryn, and she made me consider how for all the differences between André and Big Boi, they shared in the same kind of misogynoir on their first two albums. (Particularly on the song "Jazzy Belle": ". . . even Bo knew, that you got poked / like acupuncture patients while our nation is a boat.") *Misedu-*

cation had me expecting a lot more from my male heroes. A month later, OutKast dropped *Aquemini.*

Deep into the album, the song "West Savannah" ends with a skit. We hear a young black boy trying to impress his friend by calling a young black girl on the phone, three-way. When the girl answers, we hear a mama, an auntie, or a grandmama tell her to "get your ass in here." The girl tells the boy she has to go—and then the boy tells her that his friend wants some sex. The girl emphatically lets the boy know there is no way she's having sex with him, before hanging up in his face. This is where the next song, "Da Art of Storytellin' (Pt. 1)," begins.

In the first verse, Big rhymes about a sexual experience with a girl named Suzy Screw, during which he exchanges a CD and a poster for oral sex. In the second, André raps about Suzy's friend Sasha Thumper. As André's verse proceeds, he and Sasha are lying on their backs "staring at the stars above, talking bout what we gonna be when we grow up." When Dre asks Sasha what she wants to be, Sasha Thumper responds, "Alive." The song ends with the news that Sasha Thumper has overdosed after partnering with a man who treats her wrong. Here was "another black experience," as Dre would say to end another verse on the album.

Hip-hop has always embraced metafiction. In the next track—"Da Art of Storytellin' (Pt. 2)"—Big and Dre deliver a pair of verses about the last recording they'll ever create due to an environmental apocalypse. We've long had emcees rhyming about the potency of their own rhymes. But I have never heard a song attribute the end of the world to a rhyme.

DA ART OF STORYTELLIN' (A PREQUEL)

In the middle of Dre's verse, he nudges us to understand that there's something more happening in this song: "Hope I'm not over your head, but if so you will catch on later."

Big Boi alludes to the book of Revelation, mentions some ballers trying to unsuccessfully repent and make it to heaven, and then rhymes about getting his family and heading to the Dungeon, their basement studio in Atlanta—the listener can easily imagine it as a bunker—where he'll record one last song. The world is ending. He grabs the mic: "I got in the booth to run the final portion." Of course, this ending describes the very track we're hearing, thus bringing the fictional apocalypse of the song into our real world.

I was reading Octavia Butler's *Kindred* at the time *Aquemini* came out. Steeped in all that stank, I conceived of a book within a book within a book, written by a young Southern black girl whose parents disappear. "I'm a round runaway character" was the first sentence my narrator wrote. I decided that she would be an emcee, but I didn't know her name. I knew that she would tell the world that she was an ellipsis, a runaway ellipsis willing to do any and all things to stop her black Southern community from being written off the face of the earth. I scribbled these notes on the blank pages of *Kindred* while *Aquemini* kept playing in the background. By the time the song "Liberation" was done, *Long Division*, my first novel, was born.

I thought about interviewing André and Big Boi for this piece. I was going to get them to spend the night at this huge house I'm staying in this year as the writer in residence at the University of Mississippi. I planned on inviting Grandmama, too. Between the four of us, I thought we could get to the bottom of some necessary stank, and maybe play a game of "Who's Fresher?: Georgia vs. Mississippi." But the interviews fell through, and Grandmama refused to come up to Oxford because I'm the only black person she knows here, and she tends to avoid places where she doesn't know many black folks.

I kept imagining the meeting, though, and I thought a lot about what in the world I would say to Big Boi and André. As dope as they are, there's nothing I want to ask them about their art. I experienced it, and I'm thankful they extended the traditions and frequencies from whence we came. Honestly, the only thing I'd want to ask them would be about their grandmamas. I'd want to know if their grandmamas thought they were beautiful. I'd want to know how their grandmamas wanted to be loved. I'd want to know how good they were at loving their grandmamas on days when the world wasn't so kind.

The day that my grandmama came home after work without the stank of chicken guts, powder, perfume, sweat, and Coke-Cola, I knew that her time at the plant was done. On that day—when her body wouldn't let her work anymore—I knew I'd spend the rest of my life trying to honor her and make a way for her to be as fresh and remembered as she wants to be.

Due to diabetes, Grandmama moves mostly in a wheelchair these days, but she's still the freshest person in my world. Visually, I'm not so fresh. I wear the same thing every day. But I am a Southern black worker, committed to building stank-ass art rooted in honesty, will, and imagination.

This weekend, I'm going to drive down to Grandmama's house in central Mississippi. I'm going to bring my computer. I'm going to ask her to sit next to me while I finish this essay about her artistic rituals of labor vis-à-vis OutKast. I'm going to play *ATLiens* and *Aquemini* on her couch while finishing the piece, and think of every conceivable way to thank her for her stank, and for her freshness. I'm going to tell Grandmama that because of her, I know what it's like to be loved responsibly. I'm going to tell her that her love helped me listen, remember, and imagine when I never wanted to listen, remember, or imagine again. I'm going to read the last paragraph of this piece to her, and when Grandmama hugs my neck, I'm going to tell her that when no one in the world believed I was a beautiful Southern black boy, she believed. I'm going to tell Grandmama that her belief is the only reason I'm still alive, that belief in black Southern love is why we work.

Black and Blue

GARNETTE CADOGAN

"My only sin is my skin.
What did I do, to be so black and blue?"
— Fats Waller, "(What Did I Do
to Be So) Black and Blue?"

"Manhattan's streets I saunter'd, pondering."
— Walt Whitman, "Manhattan's Streets
I Saunter'd, Pondering"

My love for walking started in childhood, out of necessity. No thanks to a stepfather with heavy hands, I found every reason to stay away from home and was usually out—at some friend's house or at a street party where no minor should be—until it was too late to get public transportation. So I walked.

The streets of Kingston, Jamaica, in the 1980s were often terrifying—you could, for instance, get killed if a political henchman thought you came from the wrong neighborhood, or even if you wore the wrong color. Wearing orange showed affiliation with one political party and green with the other, and if you were neutral or traveling far from home you chose your colors well. The wrong color in the wrong neighborhood could mean your last day. No wonder, then, that my friends and the rare nocturnal passerby declared me crazy for my long late-night treks that traversed warring political zones. (And sometimes I did pretend to be crazy, shouting non sequiturs when I passed through especially dangerous spots, such as the place where thieves hid on the banks of a storm drain. Predators would ignore or laugh at the kid in his school uniform speaking nonsense.)

I made friends with strangers and went from being a very shy and awkward kid to being an extroverted, awkward one. The beggar, the vendor, the poor laborer—those were experienced wanderers, and they became my nighttime instructors; they knew the streets and delivered lessons on how to navigate and enjoy them. I imagined myself as a Jamaican Tom Sawyer, one moment sauntering down the streets to pick low-hanging mangoes that I could reach from the sidewalk, another moment hanging outside a street party with battling sound systems, each armed with speakers piled to create skyscrapers of heavy bass. These streets weren't frightening. They were full of adventure when they weren't serene. There I'd join forces with a band of merry walkers, who'd miss the last bus by mere minutes, our feet still moving as we put out our thumbs to hitchhike to spots nearer home, making jokes as vehicle after vehicle raced past us. Or I'd get lost in Mittyesque moments, my young mind imagining alternate futures. The streets had their own safety: Unlike at home, there I could be myself without fear of bodily harm. Walking became so regular and familiar that the way home became home.

The streets had their rules, and I loved the challenge of trying to master them. I learned how to be alert to surrounding dangers and nearby delights, and prided myself on recognizing telling details that my peers missed. Kingston was a map of complex, and often bizarre, cultural and political and social activity, and I appointed myself its nighttime cartographer. I'd know how to navigate away from a predatory pace, and to speed up to chat when the cadence of a gait announced friendliness. It was almost always men I saw. A lone woman walking in the middle of the night was as common a sight as Sasquatch; moonlight pedestrianism was too dangerous for her. Sometimes at night as I made my way down from hills above Kingston, I'd have the impression that the city was set on "pause" or in extreme slow motion, as that as I descended I was cutting across Jamaica's deep social divisions. I'd make my way briskly past the mansions in the hills overlooking the city, now transformed into a carpet of dotted lights under a curtain of stars, saunter by middle-class subdivisions hidden behind high walls crowned with barbed wire, and zigzag through neighborhoods of zinc and wooden shacks crammed together and leaning like a tight-knit group of limbo dancers. With my descent came an increase in the vibrancy of street life—except when it didn't; some poor neighborhoods had both the violent gunfights and the eerily deserted streets of the cinematic Wild West. I knew well enough to avoid those even at high noon.

I'd begun hoofing it after dark when I was ten years old. By thirteen I was rarely home before midnight, and some nights found me racing against dawn. My mother would often complain, "Mek yuh love street suh? Yuh born a hospital; yuh neva born a street." ("Why do you love the streets so much? You were born in a hospital, not in the streets.")

I left Jamaica in 1996 to attend college in New Orleans, a city I'd heard called "the northernmost Caribbean city." I wanted to discover—on foot, of course—what was Caribbean and what was American about it. Stately mansions on oak-lined streets with streetcars clanging by, and brightly colored houses that made entire blocks look festive; people in resplendent costumes dancing to funky brass bands in the middle of the street; cuisine—and aromas—that mashed up culinary traditions from Africa, Europe, Asia, and the American South; and a juxtaposition of worlds old and new, odd and familiar: Who wouldn't want to explore this?

On my first day in the city, I went walking for a few hours to get a feel for the place and to buy supplies to transform my dormitory room from a prison bunker into a welcoming space. When some university staff members found out what I'd been up to, they warned me to restrict my walking to the places recommended as safe to tourists and the parents of freshmen. They trotted out statistics about New Orleans's crime rate. But Kingston's crime rate dwarfed those numbers, and I decided to ignore these well-meant cautions. A city was waiting to be discovered, and I wouldn't let inconvenient facts get in the way. These American criminals are nothing on Kingston's, I thought. They're no real threat to me.

What no one had told me was that I was the one who would be considered a threat.

Within days I noticed that many people on the street seemed apprehensive of me: Some gave me a circumspect glance as they approached, and then crossed the street; others, ahead, would glance behind, register my presence, and then speed up; older white women clutched their bags; young white men nervously greeted me, as if exchanging a salutation for their safety: "What's up, bro?" On one occasion, less than a month after my arrival, I tried to help a man whose wheelchair was stuck in the middle of a crosswalk; he threatened to shoot me in the face, then asked a white pedestrian for help.

I wasn't prepared for any of this. I had come from a majority-black country in which no one was wary of me because of my skin color. Now I wasn't sure who was afraid of me. I was especially unprepared for the cops. They regularly stopped and bullied me, asking questions that took my guilt for granted. I'd never received what many of my African American friends call "The Talk": No parents had told me how to behave when I was stopped by the police, how to be as polite and cooperative as possible, no matter what they said or did to me. So I had to cobble together my own rules of engagement. Thicken my Jamaican accent. Quickly mention my college. "Accidentally" pull out my college identification card when asked for my driver's license.

My survival tactics began well before I left my dorm. I got out of the shower with the police in my head, assembling a cop-proof wardrobe. Light-colored oxford shirt. V-neck sweater. Khaki pants. Chukkas. Sweatshirt or T-shirt with my university insignia. When I walked I regularly had my identity challenged, but I also found ways to assert it. (So I'd dress Ivy League style, but would, later on, add my Jamaican pedigree by wearing Clarks Desert Boots, the footwear of choice of Jamaican street culture.) Yet the all-American sartorial choice of white T-shirt and jeans, which many police officers see as the uniform of black troublemakers, was off-limits to me—at least, if I wanted to have the freedom of movement I desired.

In this city of exuberant streets, walking became a complex and often oppressive negotiation. I would see a white woman walking toward me at night and cross the street to reassure her that she was safe. I would forget something at home but not immediately turn around if someone was behind me, because I discovered that a sudden backtrack could cause alarm. (I had a cardinal rule: Keep a wide perimeter from people who might consider me a danger. If not, danger might visit me.) New Orleans suddenly felt more dangerous than Jamaica. The sidewalk was a minefield, and every hesitation and self-censored compensation reduced my dignity. Despite my best efforts, the streets never felt comfortably safe. Even a simple salutation was suspect.

One night, returning to the house that, eight years after my arrival, I thought I'd earned the right to call my home, I waved to a cop driving by. Moments later, I was against his car in handcuffs. When I later asked him—sheepishly, of course; any other way would have asked for bruises— why he had detained me, he said my greeting had aroused his suspicion. "No one waves to the police," he explained. When I told friends of his response, it was my behavior, not his, that they saw as absurd. "Now why would you do a dumb thing like that?" said one. "You know better than to make nice with police."

A few days after I left on a visit to Kingston, Hurricane Katrina slashed and pummeled New Orleans. I'd gone not because of the storm but because my adoptive grandmother, Pearl, was dying of cancer. I hadn't wandered those streets in eight years, since my last visit, and I returned to them now mostly at night, the time I found best for thinking, praying, crying. I walked to feel less alienated—from myself, struggling with the pain of seeing my grandmother terminally ill; from my home in New Orleans, underwater and seemingly abandoned; from my home country, which now, precisely because of its childhood familiarity, felt foreign to me. I was surprised by how familiar those streets felt. Here was the corner where the fragrance of jerk chicken greeted me, along with the warm tenor and peace-and-love message of Half Pint's "Greetings," broadcast from a small but powerful speaker to at least a half-mile radius. It was as if I had walked into 1986, down to the soundtrack. And there was the wall of the neighborhood shop, adorned with the Rastafarian colors red, gold, and green along with images of local and international heroes Bob Marley, Marcus Garvey, and Haile Selassie. The crew of boys leaning against it and joshing each other were recognizable; different faces, similar stories. I was astonished at how safe the streets felt to me, once again one black body among many, no longer having to anticipate the many ways my presence might instill fear and how to offer some reassuring body language. Passing police cars were once again merely passing police cars. Jamaican police could be pretty brutal, but they didn't notice me the way American police did. I could be invisible in Jamaica in a way I can't be invisible in the United States.

Walking had returned to me a greater set of possibilities. And why walk, if not to create a new set of possibilities? Following serendipity, I added new routes to the mental maps I had made from constant walking in that city from childhood to young adulthood, traced variations on the old pathways. Serendipity, a mentor once told me, is a secular way of speaking of grace; it's unearned favor. Seen theologically, then, walking is an act of faith. Walking is, after all, interrupted falling. We see, we listen, we speak, and we trust that each step we take won't be our last, but will lead us into a richer understanding of the self and the world.

In Jamaica, I felt once again as if the only identity that mattered was my own, not the constricted one that others had constructed for me. I strolled into my better self. I said, along with Kierkegaard, "I have walked myself into my best thoughts."

When I tried to return to New Orleans from Jamaica a month later, there were no flights. I thought about flying to Texas so I could make my way back to my neighborhood as soon as it opened for reoccupancy, but my adoptive aunt, Maxine, who hated the idea of me returning to a hurricane zone before the end of hurricane season, persuaded me to come to stay in New York City instead. (To strengthen her case she sent me an article about Texans who were buying up guns because they were afraid of the influx of black people from New Orleans.)

This wasn't a hard sell: I wanted to be in a place where I could travel by foot and, more crucially, continue to reap the solace of walking at night. And I was eager to follow in the steps of the essayists, poets, and novelists who'd wandered that great city before me—Walt Whitman, Herman Melville, Alfred Kazin, Elizabeth Hardwick. I had visited the city before, but each trip had felt like a tour in a sports car. I welcomed the chance to stroll. I wanted to walk alongside Whitman's ghost and "descend to the pavements, merge with the crowd, and gaze with them." So I left Kingston, the popular Jamaican farewell echoing in my mind: "Walk good!" *Be safe on your journey,* in other words, *and all the best in your endeavors.*

I arrived in New York City, ready to lose myself in Whitman's "Manhattan crowds, with their turbulent musical chorus." I marveled at what Jane Jacobs praised as "the ballet of the good city sidewalk" in her old neighborhood, the West Village. I walked up past midtown skyscrapers, releasing their energy as lively people onto the streets, and on into the Upper West Side, with its regal Beaux Arts apartment buildings, stylish residents, and buzzing streets. Onward into Washington Heights, the sidewalks spilled over with an ebullient mix of young and old Jewish and Dominican American residents, past leafy Inwood, with parks whose grades rose to reveal beautiful views of the Hudson River, up to my home in Kingsbridge in the Bronx, with its rows of brick bungalows and apartment buildings nearby Broadway's bustling sidewalks and the peaceful expanse of Van Cortlandt Park. I went to Jackson Heights in Queens to take in people socializing around garden courtyards in Urdu, Korean, Spanish, Russian, and Hindi. And when I wanted a taste of home, I headed to Brooklyn, in Crown Heights, for Jamaican food and music and humor mixed in with the flavor of New York City. The city was my playground.

I explored the city with friends, and then with a woman I'd begun dating. She walked around endlessly with me, taking in New York City's many pleasures. Coffee shops open until predawn; verdant parks with nooks aplenty; food and music from across the globe; quirky neighborhoods with quirkier residents. My impressions of the city took shape during my walks with her.

As with the relationship, those first few months of urban exploration were all romance. The city was beguiling, exhilarating, vibrant. But it wasn't long before reality reminded me I wasn't invulnerable, especially when I walked alone.

One night in the East Village, I was running to dinner when a white man in front of me turned and punched me in the chest with such force that I thought my ribs had braided around my spine. I assumed he was drunk or had mistaken me for an old enemy, but found out soon enough that he'd merely assumed I was a criminal because of my race. When he discovered I wasn't what he imagined, he went on to tell me that his assault was my own fault for running up behind him. I blew off this incident as an aberration, but the mutual distrust between me and the police was impossible to ignore. It felt elemental. They'd enter a subway platform; I'd notice them. (And I'd notice all the other black men registering their presence as well, while just about everyone else remained oblivious to them.) They'd glare. I'd get nervous and glance. They'd observe me steadily. I'd get uneasy. I'd observe them back, worrying that I looked suspicious. Their suspicions would increase. We'd continue the silent, uneasy dialogue until the subway arrived and separated us at last.

I returned to the old rules I'd set for myself in New Orleans, with elaboration. No running, especially at night; no sudden movements; no hoodies; no objects—especially shiny ones—in hand; no waiting for friends on street corners, lest I be mistaken for a drug dealer; no standing near a corner on the cell phone (same reason). As comfort set in, inevitably I began to break some of those rules, until a night encounter sent me zealously back to them, having learned that anything less than vigilance was carelessness.

After a sumptuous Italian dinner and drinks with friends, I was jogging to the subway at Columbus Circle—I was running late to meet another set of friends at a concert downtown. I heard someone shouting and I looked up to see a police officer approaching with his gun trained on me. "Against the car!" In no time, half a dozen cops were upon me, chucking me against the car and tightly handcuffing me. "Why were you running?" "Where are you going?" "Where are you coming from?" "I said, why were you running?!" Since I couldn't answer everyone at once, I decided to respond first to the one who looked most likely to hit me. I was surrounded by a swarm and tried to focus on just one without inadvertently aggravating the others.

It didn't work. As I answered that one, the others got frustrated that I wasn't answering them fast enough and barked at me. One of them, digging through my already-emptied pockets, asked if I had any weapons, the question more an accusation. Another badgered me about where I was coming from, as if on the fifteenth round I'd decide to tell him the truth he imagined. Though I kept saying—calmly, of course, which meant trying to manage a tone that ignored my racing heart and their spittle-filled shouts in my face—that I had just left friends two blocks down the road, who were yes, sir, yes, officer, of course, officer, all still there and could vouch for me, to meet other friends whose text messages on my phone could verify that, it made no difference.

For a black man, to assert your dignity before the police was to risk assault. In fact, the dignity of black people meant less to them, which was why I always felt safer being stopped in front of white witnesses than black witnesses. The cops had less regard for the witness and entreaties of black onlookers, whereas the concern of white witnesses usually registered on them. A black witness asking a question or politely raising an objection could quickly become a fellow detainee. Deference to the police, then, was sine qua non for a safe encounter.

The cops ignored my explanations and my suggestions and continued to snarl at me. All except one of them, a captain. He put his hand on my back, and said to no one in particular, "If he was running for a long time he would have been sweating." He then instructed that the cuffs be removed. He told me that a black man had stabbed someone earlier two or three blocks away and they were searching for him. I noted that I had no blood on me and had told his fellow officers where I'd been and how to check my alibi—unaware that it was even an alibi, as no one had told me why I was being held, and of course, I hadn't dared ask. From what I'd seen, anything beyond passivity would be interpreted as aggression.

The police captain said I could go. None of the cops who detained me thought an apology was necessary. Like the thug who punched me in the East Village, they seemed to think it was my own fault for running.

Humiliated, I tried not to make eye contact with the onlookers on the sidewalk, and I was reluctant to pass them to be on my way. The captain, maybe noticing my shame, offered to give me a ride to the subway station. When he dropped me off and I thanked him for his help, he said, "It's because you were polite that we let you go. If you were acting up it would have been different."

I realized that what I least liked about walking in New York City wasn't merely having to learn new rules of navigation and socialization—every city has its own. It was the arbitrariness of the circumstances that required them, an arbitrariness that made me feel like a child again, that infantilized me. When we first learn to walk, the world around us threatens to crash into us. Every step is risky. We train ourselves to walk without crashing by being attentive to our movements, and extra-attentive to the world around us. As adults we walk without thinking, really. But as a black adult I am often returned to that moment in childhood when I'm just learning to walk. I am once again on high alert, vigilant.

Some days, when I am fed up with being considered a troublemaker upon sight, I joke that the last time a cop was happy to see a black male walking was when that male was a baby taking his first steps. On many walks, I ask white friends to accompany me, just to avoid being treated like a threat. Walks in New York City, that is; in New Orleans, a white woman in my company sometimes attracted more hostility. (And it is not lost on me that my woman friends are those who best understand my plight; they have developed their own vigilance in an environment where they are constantly treated as targets of sexual attention.) Much of my walking is as my friend Rebecca once described it: A pantomime undertaken to avoid the choreography of criminality.

Walking while black restricts the experience of walking, renders inaccessible the classic Romantic experience of walking alone. It forces me to be in constant relationship with others, unable to join the New York flaneurs I had read about and hoped to join. Instead of meandering aimlessly in the footsteps of Whitman, Melville, Kazin, and Vivian Gornick, more often I felt that I was tiptoeing in Baldwin's—the Baldwin who wrote, way back in 1960, "Rare, indeed, is the Harlem citizen, from the most circumspect church member to the most shiftless adolescent, who does not have a long tale to tell of police incompetence, injustice, or brutality. I myself have witnessed and endured it more than once." Walking as a black man has made me feel simultaneously more removed from the city, in my awareness that I am perceived as suspect, and more closely connected to it, in the full attentiveness demanded by my vigilance. It has made me walk more purposefully in the city, becoming part of its flow, rather than observing, standing apart.

But it also means that I'm still trying to arrive in a city that isn't quite mine. One definition of home is that it's somewhere we can most be ourselves. And when are we more ourselves but when walking, that natural state in which we repeat one of the first actions we learned? Walking—the simple, monotonous act of placing one foot before the other to prevent falling—turns out not to be so simple if you're black. Walking alone has been anything but monotonous for me; monotony is a luxury.

A foot leaves, a foot lands, and our longing gives it momentum from rest to rest. We long to look, to think, to talk, to get away. But more than anything else, we long to be free. We want the freedom and pleasure of walking without fear—without others' fear—wherever we choose. I've lived in New York City for almost a decade and have not stopped walking its fascinating streets. And I have not stopped longing to find the solace that I found as a kid on the streets of Kingston. Much as coming to know New York City's streets has made it closer to home to me, the city also withholds itself from me via those very streets. I walk them, alternately invisible and too prominent. So I walk caught between memory and forgetting, between memory and forgiveness.

The Condition of Black Life
Is One of Mourning

CLAUDIA RANKINE

A friend recently told me that when she gave birth to her son, before naming him, before even nursing him, her first thought was, I have to get him out of this country. We both laughed. Perhaps our black humor had to do with understanding that getting out was neither an option nor the real desire. This is it, our life. Here we work, hold citizenship, pensions, health insurance, family, friends, and on and on. She couldn't, she didn't leave. Years after his birth, whenever her son steps out of their home, her status as the mother of a living human being remains as precarious as ever. Added to the natural fears of every parent facing the randomness of life is this other knowledge of the ways in which institutional racism works in our country. Ours was the laughter of vulnerability, fear, recognition, and an absurd stuckness.

I asked another friend what it's like being the mother of a black son. "The condition of black life is one of mourning," she said bluntly. For her, mourning lived in real time inside her and her son's reality: At any moment she might lose her reason for living. Though the white liberal imagination likes

145

to feel temporarily bad about black suffering, there really is no mode of empathy that can replicate the daily strain of knowing that as a black person you can be killed for simply being black: no hands in your pockets, no playing music, no sudden movements, no driving your car, no walking at night, no walking in the day, no turning onto this street, no entering this building, no standing your ground, no standing here, no standing there, no talking back, no playing with toy guns, no living while black.

Eleven days after I was born, on September 15, 1963, four black girls were killed in the bombing of the 16th Street Baptist Church in Birmingham, Alabama. Now, fifty-two years later, six black women and three black men have been shot to death while at a Bible-study meeting at the historic Emanuel African Methodist Episcopal Church in Charleston, South Carolina. They were killed by a homegrown terrorist, self-identified as a white supremacist, who might also be a "disturbed young man" (as various news outlets have described him). It has been reported that a black woman and her five-year-old granddaughter survived the shooting by playing dead. They are two of the three survivors of the attack. The white family of the suspect says that for them this is a difficult time. This is indisputable. But for African American families, this living in a state of mourning and fear remains commonplace.

The spectacle of the shooting suggests an event out of time, as if the killing of black people with white-supremacist justification interrupts anything other than regular television programming. But Dylann Storm Roof did not create himself from nothing. He has grown up with the rhetoric and orientation of racism. He has seen white men like Benjamin F. Haskell, Thomas Gleason, and Michael Jacques plead guilty to, or be convicted of, burning Macedonia Church of God in Christ in Springfield, Massachusetts, just hours after President Obama was elected. Every racist statement he has made he could have heard all his life. He, along with the rest of us, has been living with slain black bodies.

We live in a country where Americans assimilate corpses in their daily comings and goings. Dead blacks are a part of normal life here. Dying in ship hulls, tossed into the Atlantic, hanging from trees, beaten, shot in churches, gunned down by the police, or warehoused in prisons: Historically, there is no quotidian without the enslaved, chained, or dead black body to gaze upon or to hear about or to position a self against. When blacks become overwhelmed by our culture's disorder and protest (ultimately to our own detriment, because protest gives the police justification to militarize, as they did in Ferguson), the wrongheaded question that is asked is, What kind of savages are we? Rather than, What kind of country do we live in?

In 1955, when Emmett Till's mutilated and bloated body was recovered from the Tallahatchie River and placed for burial in a nailed-shut pine box, his mother, Mamie Till Mobley, demanded his body be transported from Mississippi, where Till had been visiting relatives, to his home in Chicago. Once the Chicago funeral home received the body, she made a decision that would create a new pathway for how to think about a lynched body. She requested an open coffin and allowed photographs to be taken and published of her dead son's disfigured body.

Mobley's refusal to keep private grief private allowed a body that meant nothing to the criminal-justice system to stand as evidence. By placing both herself and her son's corpse in positions of refusal relative to the etiquette of grief, she "disidentified" with the tradition of the lynched figure left out in public view as a warning to the black community, thereby using the lynching tradition against itself. The spectacle of the black body, in her hands, publicized the injustice mapped onto her son's corpse. "Let the people see what I see," she said, adding, "I believe that the whole United States is mourning with me."

It's very unlikely that her belief in a national mourning was fully realized, but her desire to make mourning enter our day-to-day world was a new kind of logic. In refusing to look away from the flesh of our domestic murders, by insisting we look with her upon the dead, she reframed mourning as a method of acknowledgment that helped energize the civil rights movement in the 1950s and '60s.

The decision not to release photos of the crime scene in Charleston, perhaps out of deference to the families of the dead, doesn't forestall our mourning. But in doing so, the bodies that demonstrate all too tragically that "black skin is not a weapon" (as one protest poster read last year) are turned into an abstraction. It's one thing to imagine nine black bodies bleeding out on a church floor, and another thing to see it. The lack of visual evidence remains in contrast to what we saw in Ferguson, where the police, in their refusal to move Michael Brown's body, perhaps unknowingly continued where Till's mother left off.

After Brown was shot six times, twice in the head, his body was left facedown in the street by the police officers. Whatever their reasoning, by not moving Brown's corpse for four hours after his shooting, the police made mourning his death part of what it meant to take in the details of his story. No one could consider the facts of Michael Brown's interaction with the Ferguson police officer Darren Wilson without also thinking of the bullet-riddled body bleeding on the asphalt. It would be a mistake to presume that everyone who saw the image mourned Brown, but once exposed to it, a person had to decide whether his dead black body mattered enough to be mourned. (Another option, of course, is that it becomes a spectacle for white pornography: the dead body as an object that satisfies an illicit desire. Perhaps this is where Dylann Storm Roof stepped in.)

Black Lives Matter, the movement founded by the activists Alicia Garza, Patrisse Cullors, and Opal Tometi, began with the premise that the incommensurable experience of systemic racism creates an unequal playing field. The American imagination has never been able to fully recover from its white-supremacist beginnings. Consequently, our laws and attitudes have been straining against the devaluation of the black body. Despite good intentions, the associations of blackness with inarticulate, bestial criminality persist beneath the appearance of white civility. This assumption both frames and determines our individual interactions and experiences as citizens.

The American tendency to normalize situations by centralizing whiteness was consciously or unconsciously demonstrated again when certain whites, like the president of Smith College, sought to alter the language of "Black Lives Matter" to "All Lives Matter." What on its surface was intended to be interpreted as a humanist move—"aren't we all just people here?"—didn't take into account a system inured to black corpses in our public spaces. When the judge in the Charleston bond hearing for Dylann Storm Roof called for support of Roof's family, it was also a subtle shift away from valuing the black body in our time of deep despair.

Anti-black racism is in the culture. It's in our laws, in our advertisements, in our friendships, in our segregated cities, in our schools, in our Congress, in our scientific experiments, in our language, on the Internet, in our bodies no matter our race, in our communities, and, perhaps most devastatingly, in our justice system. The unarmed, slain black bodies in public spaces turn grief into our everyday feeling that something is wrong everywhere and all the time, even if locally things appear normal. Having coffee, walking the dog, reading the paper, taking the elevator to the office, dropping the kids off at school: All of this good life is surrounded by the ambient feeling that at any given moment, a black person is being killed in the street or in his home by the armed hatred of a fellow American.

The Black Lives Matter movement can be read as an attempt to keep mourning an open dynamic in our culture because black lives exist in a state of precariousness. Mourning then bears both the vulnerability inherent in black lives and the instability regarding a future for those lives. Unlike earlier black-power movements that tried to fight or segregate for self-preservation, Black Lives Matter aligns with the dead, continues the mourning, and refuses the forgetting in front of all of us. If the Rev. Martin Luther King, Jr.'s civil rights movement made demands that altered the course of American lives and backed up those demands with the willingness to give up your life in service of your civil rights, with Black Lives Matter, a more internalized change is being asked for: recognition.

The truth, as I see it, is that if black men and women, black boys and girls, mattered, if we were seen as living, we would not be dying simply because whites don't like us. Our deaths inside a system of racism existed before we were born. The legacy of black bodies as property and subsequently three-fifths human continues to pollute the white imagination. To inhabit our citizenry fully, we have to not only understand this, but also grasp it. In the words of the playwright Lorraine Hansberry, "The problem is we have to find some way with these dialogues to show and to encourage the white liberal to stop being a liberal and become an American radical." And, as my friend the critic and poet Fred Moten has written: "I believe in the world and want to be in it. I want to be in it all the way to the end of it because I believe in another world and I want to be in that." This other world, that world, would presumably be one where black living matters. But we can't get there without fully recognizing what is here.

Dylann Storm Roof's unmediated hatred of black people; Black Lives Matter; citizens' videotaping the killings of blacks; the Ferguson Police Department leaving Brown's body in the street—all these actions support Mamie Till Mobley's belief that we need to see or hear the truth. We need the truth of how the bodies died to interrupt the course of normal life. But if keeping the dead at the forefront of our consciousness is crucial for our body politic, what of the families of the dead? How must it feel to a family member for the deceased to be more important as evidence than as an individual to be buried and laid to rest?

Michael Brown's mother, Lesley McSpadden, was kept away from her son's body because it was evidence. She was denied the rights of a mother, a sad fact reminiscent of pre–Civil War times, when as a slave she would have had no legal claim to her offspring. McSpadden learned of her new identity as a mother of a dead son from bystanders: "There were some girls down there had recorded the whole thing," she told reporters. One girl, she said, "showed me a picture on her phone. She said, 'Isn't that your son?' I just bawled even harder. Just to see that, my son lying there lifeless, for no apparent reason." Circling the perimeter around her son's body, McSpadden tried to disperse the crowd: "All I want them to do is pick up my baby."

McSpadden, unlike Mamie Till Mobley, seemed to have little desire to expose her son's corpse to the media. Her son was not an orphan body for everyone to look upon. She wanted him covered and removed from sight. He belonged to her, her baby. After Brown's corpse was finally taken away, two weeks passed before his family was able to see him. This loss of control and authority might explain why after Brown's death, McSpadden was supposedly in the precarious position of accosting vendors selling T-shirts that demanded justice for Michael Brown that used her son's name. Not only were the procedures around her son's corpse out of her hands; his name had been commoditized and assimilated into our modes of capitalism.

Some of McSpadden's neighbors in Ferguson also wanted to create distance between themselves and the public life of Brown's death. They did not need a constant reminder of the ways black bodies don't matter to law enforcement officers in their neighborhood. By the request of the community, the original makeshift memorial—with flowers, pictures, notes, and teddy bears—was finally removed by Brown's father on what would have been his birthday and replaced by an official plaque installed on the sidewalk next to where Brown died. The permanent reminder can be engaged or stepped over, depending on the pedestrian's desires.

In order to be away from the site of the murder of her son, Tamir Rice, Samaria moved out of her Cleveland home and into a homeless shelter. (Her family eventually relocated her.) "The whole world has seen the same video like I've seen," she said about Tamir's being shot by a police officer. The video, which was played and replayed in the media, documented the two seconds it took the police to arrive and shoot; the two seconds that marked the end of her son's life and that became a document to be examined by everyone. It's possible this shared scrutiny explains why the police held his twelve-year-old body for six months after his death. Everyone could see what the police would have to explain away. The justice system wasn't able to do it, and a judge found probable cause to charge the officer who shot Rice with murder, while a grand jury declined to indict any of the officers involved. Meanwhile, for Samaria Rice, her unburied son's memory made her neighborhood unbearable.

Regardless of the wishes of these mothers—mothers of men like Brown, John Crawford III, or Eric Garner, and also mothers of women and girls like Rekia Boyd and Aiyana Stanley-Jones, each of whom was killed by the police—their children's deaths will remain within the public discourse. For those who believe the same behavior that got them killed if exhibited by a white man or boy would not have ended his life, the subsequent failure to indict or convict the police officers involved in these various cases requires that public mourning continue and remain present indefinitely. "I want to see a cop shoot a white unarmed teenager in the back," Toni Morrison said in April. She went on to say: "I want to see a white man convicted for raping a black woman. Then when you ask me, 'Is it over?' I will say yes." Morrison is right to suggest that this action would signal change, but the real change needs to be a rerouting of interior belief. It's an individual challenge that needs to happen before any action by a political justice system would signify true societal change.

The Charleston murders alerted us to the reality that a system so steeped in anti-black racism means that on any given day it can be open season on any black person—old or young, man, woman, or child. There exists no equivalent reality for white Americans. We can distance ourselves from this fact until the next horrific killing, but we won't be able to outrun it. History's authority over us is not broken by maintaining a silence about its continued effects.

A sustained state of national mourning for black lives is called for in order to point to the undeniability of their devaluation. The hope is that recognition will break a momentum that laws haven't altered. Susie Jackson; Sharonda Coleman-Singleton; DePayne Middleton-Doctor; Ethel Lee Lance; the Rev. Daniel Lee Simmons, Sr.; the Rev. Clementa C. Pinckney; Cynthia Hurd; Tywanza Sanders; and Myra Thompson were murdered because they were black. It's extraordinary how ordinary our grief sits inside this fact. One friend said, "I am so afraid, every day." Her son's childhood feels impossible, because he will have to be—has to be—so much more careful. Our mourning, this mourning, is in time with our lives. There is no life outside of our reality here. Is this something that can be seen and known by parents of white children? This is the question that nags me. National mourning, as advocated by Black Lives Matter, is a mode of intervention and interruption that might itself be assimilated into the category of public annoyance. This is altogether possible; but also possible is the recognition that it's a lack of feeling for another that is our problem. Grief, then, for these deceased others might align some of us, for the first time, with the living.

Know Your Rights!

EMILY RABOTEAU

On the Saturday after the Charleston church massacre wherein nine worshippers at one of the nation's oldest black churches were slaughtered during Bible study by a white gunman hoping to ignite a race war, we dragged our kids to the east side to walk them over New York City's oldest standing bridge. It seemed as good a way as any to kill a weekend afternoon. The High Bridge, which was built with much fanfare in the mid nineteenth century as part of the Croton Aqueduct system and as a promenade connecting Upper Manhattan to the Bronx over the Harlem River, had recently—and somewhat miraculously—reopened after forty-odd years of disuse. I say "miraculously" because the bridge was an infrastructure most of us had come to accept as blighted, even as some civic groups had coalesced to resurrect it. In the back of our minds that summer of 2015, as an uprising and its violent suppression raged in Missouri, was the problem of when and how to talk to our children about protecting themselves from the police.

At what age is such a conversation appropriate? By what age is it critical? How could it not be despairing? And what, precisely, should be said? The boy was four then. The girl, just two.

The day was hot. En route to the bridge we felt no reprieve from the sun, just as we'd felt no relief from the pileup of bad news about blacks being murdered with impunity. When we learned of the terror at AME Emanuel in Charleston, we had not yet recovered from the unlawful death of Freddie Gray in Baltimore, nor the shooting of Mike Brown in Ferguson, nor the chokehold death of Eric Garner in Staten Island, nor the shooting of Trayvon Martin in Florida, nor the shooting of Tamir Rice in Cleveland, to name but a few triggers of civil unrest. We weren't surprised there were no indictments in these cases, sadly enough, but we were righteously indignant. The deaths seemed to be cascading in rapid succession, each one tripping a live wire, like the feet of Muybridge's galloping horse.

The picture we were getting, and not because it was growing worse, but because our technology now exposed it, was clear and mounting evidence of discriminatory systems that don't treat or protect our citizens equally, and escalating dissent was giving rise to a movement that insists what should be evident to everyone: Black Lives Matter. There were hashtag alerts for pop-up protests in malls, die-ins on roads, and other staged acts of civil disobedience such as disruptions of white people eating their brunch. Protesters against police brutality dusted off some slogans from the civil rights era, such as "No justice—no peace!" but others were au courant: "I can't breathe," "Hands up, don't shoot!" "White silence is violence," and most poignant to me as a mother, "Is my son next?"

"It's too *hot* and my legs are too small," our son protested on the way to the bridge.

The boy was right—it was hot and getting hotter. He was tall for four but still so little. When standing at our front door, his nose just cleared the height of the doorknob. He was the same size as the pair of boys depicted in a two-panel cartoon by Ben Sargent circulating widely on my Facebook feed that summer. Both panels depict a little boy at the threshold, on the verge of stepping outdoors. The drawings are nearly identical except that the first boy is white and the second, black. "I'm goin' out, Mom!" each boy calls to a mother outside of the frame. The white boy's mother simply replies, "Put on your jacket." But the other mother's instructions comprise so intricate, leery, and vexed a warning that her words obstruct the exit: "Put on your jacket, keep your hands in sight at all times, don't make any sudden moves, keep your mouth shut around police, don't run, don't wear a hoodie, don't give them an excuse to hurt you . . ." and so on until the text in her speech bubble blurs, as in a painting by Glenn Ligon. The cartoon is titled, "Still Two Americas."

I didn't wish to be her, the mother who needed to say, "Some people will read you as black and therefore X." Why should I be the fearful mother? Nor did I covet the white mother's casual regard. I wanted to be the mother who got to say to her children, "Keep your eyes open for interesting details and take notes," as well as, "Enjoy yourselves!" on their way out the door.

But for now, I carried our sweaty girl down 173rd Street on my back while my husband led our stubborn son by the hand. You know the thermometer's popping in Washington Heights when there aren't any Dominicans out on the sidewalks playing dominoes. Nobody had yet cranked open the fire hydrants. The heat knocked out the girl as if it were a club. The boy was in a rotten mood. He demanded a drink then rejected the water we'd packed. He whined that the walk was too long, then challenged our authority in a dozen other hectoring ways until we at last arrived at Highbridge Park. There he refused to descend the hundred stairs to the bridge by flinging himself onto the asphalt with his arms and legs bent in the style of a swastika, not five feet from a dead rat. The kid's defiance bothered us for all the usual reasons a parent should find it irksome, but also because if allowed to incubate in the ghetto where we live, that defiance could get him killed.

Our son was soon coaxed down the vertiginous stairs by the magical horn of an Amtrak train on the railway beneath the bridge. He has explained to me his fierce attraction to trains and boats and vehicles in general with irritation that I didn't already know the answer: "They take you somewhere else." That's just it. From the time your children begin walking, they are moving away from you. This is as it should be, even when you can't protect them from harm with anything but the inadequate outerwear of your love.

A sweet old man in seersucker shorts stopped us at the

entrance to the bridge to make sure we appreciated the marvel of its rehabilitation. He was something of a history buff and spoke in a European accent—Greek, I think. He could recall when the bridge was shut down after falling into long decline, and the time before that when miscreants and vandals tossed projectiles over the guardrail into the polluted water below or at the traffic on the Harlem River Drive. Thanks to him, I know that the bridge was a feat of engineering originally modeled after a Roman aqueduct, siphoning water from Westchester County through pipes beneath its walkway into the city, enabling New Yorkers to enjoy their first indoor plumbing (including the flush toilet). The old man never thought he'd live to see the day when the High Bridge was back in business, and was proud that the citizen-led campaign to reopen it had succeeded. "This bridge changed everything," the old man said in wonderment, as if the relic was a truer paean to empire than the skyscrapers twinkling in the skyline far to the south of us—the Chrysler Building, the former Citicorp Center, and the spire of the Empire State. Dutifully, we paraded across to the Bronx. Maybe it was because I so admired the old man's perspective, attuned as it was to a less conspicuous wonder of the world, that on our return trip home I noticed a mural I could have sworn had not been there before.

"KNOW YOUR RIGHTS!" the mural trumpeted in capital letters. How had it escaped my attention? The artwork covered a brick wall abutting the twenty-four-hour Laundromat

Artist: Nelson Rivas, aka Cekis. Washington Heights, Upper Manhattan, Wadsworth Avenue and 174th Street, 2009. "If you are detained or arrested by a police officer, demand to speak with an attorney and don't tell them anything until an attorney is present." "Ud. no tiene que estar de acuerdo con un chequeo de si mismo, su carro o su casa. No trate físicamente de parar la policía. Solo diga que ud. no da permiso para el chequeo. Tienes el derecho de no aceptarlo." "Ud. tiene el derecho de observar y filmar actividades policiales."

I passed every weekday morning on the walk to the children's day care. A vision of tropical blues, it splashed out from the gritty gray surroundings, creating an illusion of depth. My eyes drank it in.

This mural operates like a comic strip in panels marrying image and text. In the first panel, a youngster is carded by a law enforcement official. In the second, a goateed man in a baseball cap is being handcuffed. In the third, a group of citizens stare evenly outward. One of them wears a look of disgust, and a T-shirt that says, "4th Amendment," a sly allusion to the part of our constitution that protects us against unreasonable search and seizure without probable cause. Another holds his cell phone aloft to record what is happening on the street. "You have the right to film and observe police activity," the mural states in Spanish, appropriate for a neighborhood where Spanish is the dominant language and where young men of color are regularly stopped and frisked by the police. In the lower left-hand corner the Miranda rights are paraphrased in English.

My first instinct was to take a picture of the mural so that I could carry it with me in my pocket. I was grateful for it, not only as a thing of beauty on the gallery of the street, but also as a kind of answer to the question that had been troubling us—how to inform our children about the harassment they might face. The mural struck me as an act of love for the people who would pass it by. I understood why it had been made, and why it had been made here in the hood next to a Laundromat as opposed to on Fifth Avenue next to Henri Bendel, Tiffany's, or Saks. It was armor against the cruelty of the world. It was also a salve, to reclaim physical and psychic space. I wondered who had done it.

After some Internet sleuthing I discovered the painter was a Chilean artist who goes by the tag name Cekis, and that this mural was the first of several public artworks commissioned by a coalition of grassroots organizations called People's Justice for Community Control and Police Accountability. The other Know Your Rights murals were spread out across four of New York City's five boroughs (excluding Staten Island, where a great number of cops live) in poor neighborhoods most plagued by police misconduct. For the rest of that summer and into the fall, I photographed as many of them as I could, like a magpie collecting bright things for her nest.

The second mural I shot was in central Harlem.

As with the mural in Washington Heights, I chose to capture a passerby in the frame, to give a sense of scale but with the intent to preserve the subject's anonymity. Thrown against a sharp white background, the man in Harlem appears in silhouette, his beard like Thelonious Monk's, his shadow extending from his feet, and the shadow of the fire escape above him slanting down against the mural like the bars of a cage. A woman depicted in the mural's foreground holds a bullhorn to her mouth. A portion of the text reads, "Write down the officer's badge number, name, and/or other identifying info. You don't have to answer any questions from police." Her advice is specifically targeted to those at risk of being stopped and frisked.

© Emily Raboteau

Lead Artist: Sophia Dawson. *Know Your Rights*, Harlem, Upper Manhattan, 138th Street and Adam Clayton Powell Jr. Boulevard, 2013. "Write down the officer's badge #, name, and/or other identifying info." "Get medical attention if needed and take pictures of injuries." "You don't have to answer any questions from police. When they approach, say, 'Am I being detained, or am I free to go?' If they detain you, stay silent + demand a lawyer. A frisk is only a pat down. If police try to do more than that say loudly, 'I do not consent to this search.'" "You have the right to observe, photograph, record, and film police activity."

Stop-and-frisk policing was implemented in New York as part of an increased trend of enforcement that began in response to rising crime and the crack cocaine epidemic of the 1980s and '90s. The technique disproportionately affects young men of color. (From 2004 through 2012, African Americans and Hispanics were subject to nearly 90 percent of the 4.4 million stop-and-frisk actions despite constituting only about half of the city's population.) In black and Latino neighborhoods like Harlem and Washington Heights, residents often view the police, a force ostensibly there to protect them, with mistrust and fear. In 2013, the year the Harlem mural was made, a federal court judged the use of stop-and-frisk tactics to be excessive and unconstitutional. Since then, their use has declined. Critics of reducing the practice predicted a rise in crime. Instead, overall crime has dropped. I would like to believe these statistics mean it's growing slightly safer for my children to walk.

Yul-san Liem, who works for one of the activist organizations that makes up People's Justice, explained to me that the murals were financed by the Center for Constitutional Rights. "Visual art communicates differently than the written or spoken word," she commented. "By creating Know Your Rights murals, we seek to bring important information directly to the streets where it is needed the most, and in a way that is memorable and visually striking."

People's Justice formed in 2007 in the wake of the NYPD killing of the unarmed black man Sean Bell the day before his wedding. "It wasn't an isolated incident," Liem lamented, recalling the 1999 killing of Amadou Diallo, the unarmed black man shot forty-one times by police, and the assault of Abner Louima, who was sodomized by police with a broom handle in 1997, allegedly told to "Take that, nigger!" Liem said, "Our original goal was to highlight the systemic nature of police violence in communities of color. We've taken a proactive approach to empowerment that includes organizing neighborhood-based Cop Watch teams and outreach that uses public art as a means of education. It's about shifting culture and creating hope."

Maybe that's what I was scavenging for. Hope. I like how Emily Dickinson defined it—"the thing with feathers."

The third mural that I shot was in Bushwick, Brooklyn. I had difficulty finding it, in part because Bushwick is a neighborhood of murals but also because Liem had given me bum directions. I lost myself in the rainbow spectacle of street art. There was Nelson Mandela on a wall overlooking the parking lot of a White Castle, but where was the mural I sought? I asked a group of kids in Catholic school uniforms if they knew where I could find it. They all claimed to know the Know Your Rights mural, but none could give me an exact address. Either it was somewhere down Knickerbocker Avenue or else it was located in the opposite direction past three or four schoolyards and a car wash. In the end, one girl kindly volunteered to walk me there. She wore a purple backpack, braces on her teeth, and a gold name necklace that said coincidentally (or not) "Esperanza." Esperanza told me with excitement that she'd be getting an

Artist: Dasic Fernández. *Know Your Rights,* Bushwick, Brooklyn, Irving Avenue and Gates Avenue, 2011. "If you are harassed by police, write down the officer's badge number, name, and/or other identifying information. Get medical attention if you need it and take pictures of any injuries." "All students have the right to attend school in a safe, secure, non-threatening and respectful learning environment in which they are free from harassment." "No tenant can be evicted from their apartment without being taken to housing court." "Si ud. es detenido o arrestado por un policía, pida hablar con un abogado immediatamente. No diga nada hasta que tiene un abogado presente." "Owners are required by law to keep their buildings safe, well maintained and in good repair. If not, call 911."

iPhone like mine for her thirteenth birthday. After peram-
bulating for a half an hour we finally located the mural in an
overgrown lot behind a chain-link fence. We'd had so many
false sightings at that point that I sensed it was part of the
girl's mental, rather than physical, landscape. It rose out of
the weeds in pastel shades like an enormous Easter egg. "I
love this one," she confessed. "It's so *big*."

As with the murals in Washington Heights and Harlem, the
text of the Bushwick mural exhorts the viewer to watch and
film police activities. This time the message is underscored by
a figure in the foreground who points to her enormous eye as
if to say, "Watch out. Keep your eyes open." A man directly
behind her uses his phone to film a police officer making an
arrest in the mural's background. The phone is configured as
a weapon for social change. The teenager that I photograph
walking past the mural is also on the phone. Though she
appears oblivious to the mural, she also appears, in the context
of my photo, to be wielding a tool. That is, the phone distracts
her from being present but she could also deploy its camera at
any moment to record what's happening on the street.

The fourth mural that I shot was painted on a corrugated fence
in Long Island City, Queens, across from the Ravenswood
housing projects. On my way through the projects I passed
a barefoot lady in a church hat pushing a stroller full of cans.
She was involved in a heated argument over a Metrocard
with a man invisible to me. In the middle of an invective she
stopped to tell me he was a lying thief. "I believe you," I

Artist: Dasic Fernández. *Know Your Rights,* Long Island City, Queens, Thirty-fifth Avenue and Twelfth Street, 2012. "If you are HARRASSED by police, write down the officer BADGE number, name and/or other identifying information. Take PICTURES of any INJURIES." "Ud no tiene que estar de aquerdo con un chequeo de si mismo, su carro o su casa. No pare físicamente a la policía. Diga que ud. no da permiso para el chequeo."

said, emphatically. "He's a jerk." We smiled at each other. She returned to her dispute and I went on my way.

"If you are HARASSED by police . . ." the Long Island City mural advises, ". . . take PICTURES of any INJURIES." Again, the mural is a backdrop to walking but this time, because it consists entirely of text, the message is even starker. A woman is about to cross the street. I don't know where she's going, or what she's looking at. She may be checking for oncoming traffic or reading the warning on the mural. Her braids swing across her back as her sneaker approaches the curb. My friend the writer Garnette Cadogan has said, "Walking is among the most dignified of human activities." But here, the woman's simple dignified act of walking, whether home from work or school, or to the bodega for a carton of milk, is erupted by the somber memo that hangs in the background. The public space feels contested and even traumatic because of the public art. The intersection looks hazardous, like something is about to hit her.

The fifth mural I shot was in Bedford-Stuyvesant, the swiftly gentrifying Brooklyn neighborhood made famous by Spike Lee's landmark film *Do the Right Thing*. In fact, the Bed-Stuy mural directly references that movie by depicting the character Radio Raheem. At the start of the movie, Radio Raheem blasts Public Enemy's "Fight the Power" from his boombox like a reveille. Near the movie's end, he's choked to death by a nightstick-wielding cop—a pivotal plot point that incites a riot, much like the uprisings that followed the Rodney King

© Emily Raboteau

Artist: Trust Your Struggle (collective), *Trust Your Struggle*, Bedford Stuyvesant, Brooklyn, Marcus Garvey Boulevard and Macdonough Street, 2010. "Justice or Just Us." "LOVE/HATE." "Stay calm and in control. Don't get into an argument. Remember officer's badge and patrol car number. Don't resist, even if you believe you're innocent. You don't have to consent to be searched. Try to find a witness & get their name & contact. Anything you say can be used against you. Know Your Rights. Trust Your Struggle. Spread love. It's the Brooklyn way. Didn't pass the bar, but know a little bit; enough that you won't illegally search N.Y."

verdict in Los Angeles, and the Freddie Gray verdict in Baltimore, and the Michael Brown verdict in Ferguson, which reverberated across the country like so many waves of heat.

In New York, I remember the Ferguson protesters took to the streets chanting, "Whose streets? Our streets!" I myself was drawn to the vortex of 125th Street, where I shot pictures of the crowd swarming toward the Triborough Bridge. I paused there at the edge of my own reason sometime before midnight to return to my children, but the mob pushed on as far as the tollbooths on the Manhattan side, succeeding in shutting the bridge down. It felt so logical an impulse, to act unruly in the face of misrule. Yet this impulse is what the Bed-Stuy mural admonishes against.

Radio Raheem's fist is the focal point of the mural, adorned with its gold "LOVE" knuckleplate. The mural, dominated by the color red, cautions the viewer to "Stay calm and in control. Don't get into an argument . . . Don't resist, even if you believe you're innocent."

The man I photograph walking past the love punch wears paint-splattered work boots, a headcloth over his dreadlocks, and earphones. I wonder what he's listening to. Perhaps because he's distracted by his music, he's unaware that I've shot him with my phone.

So was the woman in the Bronx, where I took my sixth and final picture. She was too absorbed by the screen of her device to notice me, though if she looked my way, she would have seen that I too was operating my phone. My posture mir-

Artist: Dasic Fernández. *Know Your Rights,* Hunts Point, Bronx, Barretto Street and Garrison Avenue, 2012. "You have the right to watch & film police activities." "If you are detained or arrested by a police officer, demand to speak with an attorney and don't say anything until attorney is present."

rored the person in the mural who films a plainclothes police officer cuffing a man over the hood of a car. I had to wait over an hour to get this shot because a belligerent drunk pissing on the sidewalk refused to get out of the frame. Finally, he zipped up and drifted off beneath the Bruckner Expressway. Of all the neighborhoods I traversed, Hunts Point felt the roughest. On the long walk to the Point from the elevated 2 train through the red light district, I was surveyed with interest. I felt that if I wasn't mindful, someone down on his luck might succeed in snatching my phone. Yet I stayed planted by the mural, looking for something concrete.

The phone in the Hunts Point mural is almost as tall as the woman walking beneath it, its screen the approximate size of her handbag. In the screenshot we see repeated the nested image of the plainclothes police officer cuffing a man over the hood of the car. The dizzying effect of the mural is to put the viewer in the perspective of the photographer.

I have fallen into the mural or rather the mural has sucked me in. I am the third dimension; the watcher. I am the photographer with the phone in her hand. So, potentially, is the passerby, though in this context her posture is also a reminder that passivity has its cost. The woman is about to step out of my frame. For now she is caught, as in a web, by the shadows of power lines and trees. The text behind her echoes that of the first mural I shot on the streets of Washington Heights: "If you are detained or arrested by a police officer, demand to speak with an attorney and don't say anything until the attorney is present."

It was as if the text were on a loop. I'd begun to feel I was moving in circles and so I stopped to take stock of my pictures, scrolling backward. Though the style of each mural was distinct, the message was the same. Somebody loves you enough to try to keep you safe by informing you of your rights. The murals' insistence on those rights, which the citizens of our nation don't yet equally enjoy, reminded me that like the High Bridge, the Constitution is just another lofty infrastructure in need of rehabilitation. Such changes do occur, it seems. Were it not for the fact that I shot them in different locales, I felt I could craft a zoetrope of the passersby to show my children. The many walkers would appear unified as one—even if at times that walker was a woman or a man, or black, or brown, or old or young—advancing toward one steady goal. "Look how marvelous," I would say of the moving image. And if my children asked me where the walker was going, I would answer, "To the bridge."

© Emily Raboteau

Composite Pops

MITCHELL S. JACKSON

How does a fatherless boy spell *father*?

One answer is in the video of a poet who monologues about a dream in which he's a child contestant in a spelling bee. For the win, he has to spell the word *father*. He proceeds to spell the word *m-o-t-h-e-r*. Then when the spellmaster says he's "incorrect," he launches into a rant about absentee fathers and womanizing men and maternal strength . . .

While plenty mothers in the world deserve the most huge hurrahs, what I want to say to this poet and other like minds is this: no matter how much we lambast men and high-note praise women, a woman maketh a father not.

Yes, ours is indeed a revolutionary era of gender fluidness and sexual equality and girls doubtless need dads too—I repeat: girls need their dads. No way no how no day would I try to diminish or worse negate the role of a dad in his daughter's life. No one, and that includes humans, saints, and extraterrestrials, could convince me that my princess's life would be better off without me in it. However, just as there are some aspects of being a female that my daughter's mother is more equipped to guide her through, there are aspects of being a male that I hope I have helped my son navigate in a way that only I could.[1]

This is my beating heart: boys need fathers.

Boys need fathers—period, exclamation point.

And if a boy is not blessed with a father or gifted with a dynamic stand-in then he must find ways to make one. He must identify the father*ish* men in his life, find what he needs from them, and compose one.

It is an act of necessity, and I should know. My mother was not far along into her nineteenth year when she had me by a man who lived no more than a bike ride away but was absent for my first decade of life.[2] To say I had no father, though, is a half-truth. To say my mother was my father would be a sentimental-ass lie. I had a father, and I had one because I made one. Or rather I composed a father from the men at hand, brothers who kept me long before Obama made it a project.[3]

There was my mother's long-term boyfriend Big Chris, my maternal grandfather Sam, my maternal uncle Anthony, my paternal uncle Henry, and at long last my biological father, Wesley. If you asked me to spell *father*, I could turn their names into one long-ass portmanteau.

Or I might just say "p-o-p-s."

Pops was a group of men who provided a loving example of what it would soon enough mean to be a man. Pops nurtured me. Bestowed me with his wisdom. Pushed me to nuance the way I saw the world. He inspired me to dream. He tended my harms. He made sure I knew it was in me to surpass him.

BIG CHRIS

Far as I knew growing up my biological father was a ghost by the time I was born. By the time I was a year old, my mother had been heart-throbbed by a man named Big Chris. Big Chris was a recent parolee—bank robbery, what a dreamer!—and a neophyte/soon-to-be-prosperous pimp, but also a smart, witty, compassionate man whose jokes could give you stomachaches. My mother had two boys by Big Chris and stayed with him until just before I reached double digits. For years after he left, he would swing through trying to rekindle his and my mother's faded love or else connect with his boys, and without a doubt, whether Big Chris and my mom were an official couple or not, I was one of those boys. The man never treated me one bit different from the sons of his seed. The naysayers can knock how he hustled his bread and meat, but that don't change the fact that Big Chris was the one who showed me the value and impact of a father's love, that family often had nothing to do with genetics. This was a lesson he taught me in life and in death.

In September 2009, I got a call from Big Chris's daughter— my oldest sister—saying that he was sick and that I should fly out to Phoenix to see him. In the span of a few days, she went from prodding me to make it out soon, to imploring me to come ASAP if I wanted to see him alive. The next day I was on a flight, bracing for the worst and praying against it. My flight landed heartstroke hours later and while passengers were grabbing their bags, I turned on my cell phone to a fusillade of texts: from my mother, from my brothers, from my sister—all warning me Big Chris had died. My big sister picked me up from the airport, and tried to console me with Dad's near-to-last words: "I've got to hold on. I've got to hold on so I can see Mitch." The story didn't console me in the moment, but later, much later, when the grief begrudged me room to breathe, Dad's near-to-last words confirmed for me the bond that we'd shared, reaffirmed that I would forever be one of his boys, that our kinship was deeper than DNA.

SAM

My maternal grandfather, Sam Jackson, Jr., rose every day for thirty-plus years to go to the same job. He attends church every Sunday—and arrives on time all the time. He pays his bills and his tithes. He represents at neighborhood rallies and community meetings. He bought and has lived in the same house since the '70s, lived there with his wife until she died, lives there with a new wife now. Granddad or Dad, as I call him, rescued us—my mom and her boys— countless times with funds because the electric company put an apartment of ours on eclipse or the rent had somehow vamoosed out of my mom's purse. Granddad moved me into his house for my last two years of high school, this after I ran away from my biological father's house, after I'd made it clear to all concerned adults that I couldn't be trusted under the charge of my half-paralyzed great-grandmother. Me, Granddad, and my cousin-brother Jesse ate breakfast together in his kitchen damn near every weekday.[4] Granddad sat in the bleachers at my home and away high school hoop games and kept full stats. He chided me to mow the lawn and take out the trash and repaid me by spotting me the bucks I needed to hang with my homeboys on Friday nights. He never once bemoaned being my caretaker, as I imagined he had a right to, not even after he had to slap spit from me for the class-A house crime of sneaking girls into my basement bedroom.[5] Granddad has modeled what it means to be a stand-up dude, what it means to honor your commitments, what it means to shoulder your obligations and your burdens without gripe.

ANTHONY (ANT)

My maternal uncle Ant wore some version of a Jheri curl well past the great epoch of Jheri curls. Furthermore, Ant's held on to his almost-a-high-school-All-American story for generations, a legend I've heard told so often at family dinners, that sometimes I go ahead and tell it myself. Let Ant or me tell it, the judges clocked him at 9.7, 9.6, and 9.5 in the 100-yard sprint at a district track meet, but if they had given him an official time of 9.5 instead of 9.6, he "would've been an All-American that year."

Ant's story is a tendon to what happened to me in sixth grade, the only year I ever competed on a track team. That year, I'd taken second place in the district meet to a rival who had been putting a whooping on me all season. Ant attended that meet and was disappointed right along with me. He could've let me play a defeatist, but instead he took it upon himself to train me for the city championship, swooping me afternoons after school and teaching me to run on my toes and lean forward and lengthen my stride, drilling into my porous brain the idea that I could beat anyone as long as I used good form and believed. The championships rolled around a couple of weeks later and sure enough I was lined up against my rival in the 100-meter final. Pow! We took off and by midway through the race I was losing in slo-mo and heard my heart scream no, no, nooooooooooo. Then by some kind of Prefontaine magic I heard Ant screaming, "REACH, nephew! REACH!" above all other voices, and reach I did on the way to winning the race with a slight cushion. You should have seen Ant afterward, rejoicing as if, at once, I'd won Olympic gold and salved his All-American wound. Thanks to Ant, I had my first taste of being a champion in public, of realizing that with assiduousness and self-confidence, my impossible was possible. For sure he was a father that day, one who'd pushed me to succeed where he'd failed, to be bolder, bigger, stronger, best.

HENRY

Somewhere in my random collection of family archives is a hubris-building copy of a news feature on my paternal uncle Henry titled, "Superman in Solitary: Oregon's Big-gest Dope Dealer Tells All." The story details Uncle Henry's 1970s to mid-'80s evolution from car thief and pimp to drug kingpin. The article was straight-up inspiration, though, full disclosure, I didn't know Uncle Henry at all during the days of him hustling enough funds to buy a plane and Rolls-Royce. In fact, we spent almost no time together until right after I graduated high school, which was the summer I decided that being a devoted part-time dope dealer was the best present way for me to make a living. Keep in mind, this was decades past Uncle Henry's gilded heyday, well into the age of him being a shyster and ardent addict, and though I knew about his fall, I was beguiled by the lore, was hungry to profit from secrets I was sure he owned. So one day my older brother—a fellow neophyte dope dealer—and me tracked down Uncle Henry at the apartment of another uncle and pressed him for what in effect was a session of Drug Dealing 101. Uncle Henry, ever the capitalist, obliged us a lesson for a few shards of our dope. Can't recall every-thing he said, but one point will stick with me till I'm dust: "The fast nickel beats the slow twenty." My uncle went on to explain that while we waited forever for a twenty sale, we could've sold umpteen fives, which meant to me that what I dreamed of would not arrive in a windfall but would accrue one small sale at a time. It's easy to make the case that Uncle Henry was undermining my brother and me, but the way I see it, his advice had less to do with corrupting our youth or sabotaging our gleaming futures, and more to do with the munificence of exposing us to a maxim that had grand effect for him. Because he knew that no matter what we did, we would need to learn how to hustle—to reimagine paths to success—that hustling was vital to young black boys, that without it we were destined to be failed black men. Though I never made hundreds of thousands nor had the misfortune of being the local drug kingpin, Uncle Henry's lecture and legacy helped convince me that I had hustle in my blood, and please believe me when I tell you, I've been a hustler ever since.

WESLEY

Ten—that's how old I was when I met my biological father. One of my most significant memories of him occurred not too long after when his wife, oldest son, two daughters, and I road-tripped to visit Disneyland, Sea World, and a few Californian family members. One of those relatives lived in an apartment complex with a pool—a pool! We all changed into swimming gear and headed out to the pool, where my dad and my brother and sisters began having a grand old time swimming and playing in the water and goading me to get in while I gallivanted *around* the pool and at most teased my foot in the shallow end once or twice. My trepidation was for good reason as this was circa '85, arguably the height of a certain highwater-pants and rhine-stone-glove-wearing pop star, and I had a Jheri curl befit-ting a kid who claimed to certain credulous classmates that I was a not-so-distant cousin. Or let me put it like this: young

Mitch Jackson was not about to get his MJ-esque dew wet nor—the extent of my swimming skills at the time was a hella-weak doggy paddle—was I about to risk my life. But my biological father flexed contrary designs by creeping up behind me and scooping me in the air and tossing me in the pool. He didn't flinch while I flailed and screamed and gulped mouthfuls of overchlorinated water. He said something to me that I can't remember but that my subconscious must've heard because soon I calmed and got my curly head above the surface, and stayed in the pool and had a damn good day frolicking with my father, brother, and sisters—aka the Johnsons. The message of that day took years to reveal itself to me: "Troubled water or not, you best learn to swim. 'Cause when your young-ass get to drowning, I may not be moved to rescue." That message, by the way, I now count as an act of stern beneficence.

Not one of the men I mentioned has existed in my life beyond the reach of critique. Oh yes, I comprehend flaws. But their foibles weren't the crux of what I used to build. I must say, too, that they were much more than mentors. Mentors teach you a skill. Fathers teach you to live. Your mentor's role can remain static. Your father's role must evolve. A mentor's direction might be free of deep feeling. A father's guidance must be rooted in love.

Who I am now is who I must be: a flawed human striving to live in a state of becoming. Along the way I've discovered a thing or more about myself: that who and how I love is not dictated by law or blood, that being a constant presence is as much a part of being a man as almost anything else, that what I want must be earned, that I can win and win I will, that there's hustle in my genes, that either I swim or drown and there is no one more important to that outcome than me.

Now here I am the father of two children, trying my all-out damnedest to mind the lessons of my beloved composite, all the while feeling encouraged by the fact I know they're rooting for me to best the job they did.

Thank. You. Pops.

• • •

1. Praise be to the gender politicians. By male and female I mean cisgendered male and female—the Latin prefix *cis* means "on the same side"—i.e., men and women whose gender identity is aligned with the gender they were assigned by birth.

2. For my DNA dad's sake, I must note that the absoluteness of his early absence is a point of dispute.

3. Obama (BO) is the latest exemplar—a total of twelve were either abandoned or lost their biological fathers when they were young—of a president whose life confirms how efficacious it is to compose a composite. It's damn near folklore now, how Barack Hussein Obama, Sr., had bounced on his wife and BO by the time he was a toddler, how his mother spent time in Seattle, remarried in Hawaii, took young BO to live with her new husband in Indonesia, but sent him back to the Aloha State to live with her parents around the time he entered the fifth grade. One of BO's composites thereafter, if nothing else for the fact that he assumed the role of his long-term primary caretaker until he went off to college, was his maternal grandfather Stanley Dunham (no shade to Stanley's wife's role in co-parenting her grandson). Stanley was also the one who introduced BO to the man who just might own the

title of Most Controversial of all presidential composites: a libertine, ex-journalist, poet, and Communist associate named Frank Marshall Davis, a man who became especially infamous during BO's first campaign when conspiracy theorists claimed Davis was his biological father. The truth, though, as confirmed by BO in his memoir, is that Davis helped shape his views on racial identity, race relations, and social justice. Davis was a part of BO's life but for a handful of years, but I'm calling him a composite for his impact. For example, though this next point may be a stretch (then again, so was a black man being elected the leader of the free world), remnants of Davis's radical thought can be found in the socialist-leaning legislation that is Obama Care. From the last to the first. George Washington (GW) lost his father, Augustine (Augustine's people called him Gus), when he was eleven. From that point, GW's older half-brother Lawrence Washington became his surrogate father. Answer me this: What would America look like if GW hadn't followed Lawrence into the military and politics (Lawrence fought in the War of Jenkins Ear and was later elected to Virginia's House of Burgesses)? Lawrence christened the Mount Vernon estate (or should we call it a plantation?), and GW paid homage to his beloved older brother when it was in his sole possession by hanging only his portrait in his study. GW and BO are notable for being the first and last, but the list between them includes Thomas Jefferson (TJ), who lost his father at thirteen and found a mentor in the philosophy professor William Small when he entered William and Mary College a few years later. Smith fostered in TJ a great appreciation for diverse disciplines and also a love of Enlightenment thinkers. He also introduced TJ to the politician and law professor George Wythe—the man who became TJ's unofficial political and cultural mentor—as much a composite as any man was for the future president. How amazing it must've been for an ambitious young TJ to sit around a supper table discussing politics and culture with Small, Wythe, and a governor. How fortunate TJ was to have been given the chance to later study law (there were no law schools in colonial America) with Wythe, and have that apprenticeship that included history, philosophy, and ethics. If you're looking for the lasting influence of TJ's composite, you need look no further than the ideals and language of the most important document in American history. The list of presidents who built composites also includes Gerald Ford (GF)—he was born Leslie King, Jr.—whose mother, Dorothy, divorced his biological father, Leslie King, Sr., on the grounds of "extreme cruelty" when her son was five months old. GF's biological father was the son of the millionaire businessman Charles Henry King, but that didn't stop him from bolting out of state (so much for broke pockets being the impetus for a deadbeat dad) and, as rumor had it, colluding with his father to skirt alimony and child-support judgments. Lucky for baby GF that Dorothy met Gerald Ford, Sr., a couple of years later. Ford Sr. wasn't no slouch. He became a successful businessman, was a church vestryman, a Mason, and later a local politician. He married Dorothy, adopted her young son, christened him a junior, and was, in GF's words, "kind, fair, and firm." Ford Sr. and Dorothy, who had three more boys together, didn't mention to GF that Ford Sr. was not his biological father. GF didn't find that out until his biological father showed up at his high school job. But years and years later, in a letter GF dictated from the Oval Office, you can see how that visit did little to change his mind about his beloved composite: "I loved and was guided in life by the only father I ever had—Gerald R. Ford Sr. There was never any longing on my part to seek family outside of the one in which I was raised with such love, tenderness, and happiness."

4. When my cousin-brother Jesse's mother was murdered, he went to live with my great-grandparents for a time, but when he hit the first grade, he moved in with my granddad and lived with him until he became a legal adult. My granddad parenting Jesse is yet another hashmark in the ledger of why he deserves my love, respect, and admiration.

5. The backstory: this occurred after I'd been caught on occasion with naked to half-naked girls in my basement bedroom. The scene: my granddad's house sits beside an alley, and there's a park bench at the opening of the alley. The action: this particular day

my granddad came home early from work and spotted me sitting on that park bench with a girl whose name I couldn't name now if you paid me, but whose face I will never forget. By sitting I mean that I was leaned into her ear whispering the sweet nothings I hoped would lead to her knickknacks. She and I had not been in the house, though, so I was miffed when my granddad stopped his Buick in the alley and furied over to us. "Hey, Dad, this is—" and before I could finish, he barked, "What did I tell you?! What did I tell you about this?!" and slapped the sound of a firework out of my cheek. He breathed over me for a moment or two and stomped back to his idling ride and meandered it into the garage. The girl's mouth was agape when I got up the courage to look at her. You should go, I said. She shook her head yes. You should go now, I said, and she rose and headed up the alley. She and I never spoke another word to each other after that day. These years later, I realize it was a testament to how much I love my granddad that it never dawned on me to curse him under my breath or consider running away like I damn sure would've if instead it was my DNA dad who'd struck me. Pretty sure I never snuck another girl into the basement either—which spells mission accomplished for Sam Jackson, Jr., excuse me, mission accomplished for Dad.

PART III

JUBILEE

Theories of Time and Space

NATASHA TRETHEWEY

You can get there from here, though
there's no going home.

Everywhere you go will be somewhere
you've never been. Try this:

head south on Mississippi 49, one-
by-one mile markers ticking off

another minute of your life. Follow this
to its natural conclusion—dead end

at the coast, the pier at Gulfport where
rigging of shrimp boats are loose stitches

in a sky threatening rain. Cross over
the man-made beach, twenty-six miles of sand

dumped on the mangrove swamp—buried
terrain of the past. Bring only

what you must carry—tome of memory,
its random blank pages. On the dock

where you board the boat for Ship Island
someone will take your picture:

the photograph—who you were—
will be waiting when you return.

This Far: Notes on Love and Revolution

DANIEL JOSÉ OLDER

August 2015

Dear Nastassian:

You told me to write this essay to our future children, but I'm writing to you instead. You said to tell them about how their mom worried, how she wasn't sure if it was a good idea bringing black life into a world that doesn't value it, but that she landed on hope amidst all the despair. *Tell them*, you said, *about why their father does the work he does, what kind of world you hope to help build for them.*

And I will, love, I will. But this moment right now—the night is quiet and I write while you sleep—this moment with all its weight and responsibility, this turning point in the world and our lives, is ours, and these words are for you.

Three weeks ago we rode through the midnight streets of Kingston, Jamaica, past shacks and gas stations, jerk chicken cookouts and quicky motels, to the airport and this new life together. Our Twitter feeds and the national news were filled with updates on Sandra Bland, the latest black life destroyed while in police custody, the most recent name to become a hashtag. Every time her deathlike mugshot flashed across the screen I felt an ache detonate in me. It's an ache many of us have become intimate with over the past year, as the hard work of protesters brings light to each new state-sanctioned murder. It recedes and then returns, compounded by the tragedy of how familiar it feels to mourn a stranger.

In college, I scribbled a quote from Eqbal Ahmad in the back of my notebook: ". . . this out-administration occurs when you identify the primary contradiction of your adversary and expose that contradiction . . . to the world at large." Ahmad wrote those words in reference to global struggles against empire, and trapped as I was just then, and probably always will be, in some wordy labyrinth between the future and past, the sentence settled somewhere in my brain and caught fire.

In a way, these words infer the same conclusion as the other quotes I'd copied around it: that art is a creator and a destroyer and no less a player in the great stage of the world than politics or violence. "It is in the nexus of representation, words, and space," Michel Foucault wrote, "that the destiny of peoples is silently formed." Or the Syrian poet Nizar Qabbani: "Our deliverance is in drawing with words."

But Mr. Ahmad dispenses with the formality of arguing the power of representation, and jumps directly into strategy. Unlike so many of the texts we read in college, this passage is not concerned with making people comfortable or rehashing basic truths that are deemed controversial only because they agitate overprotected egos. "I argued that armed struggle," Eqbal Ahmad writes at the beginning of that paragraph, "is less about arms and more about organization, that a successful armed struggle proceeds to out-administer the adversary and not out-fight him." Ahmed is concerned with victory, which is to say, survival.

It's been a year since Officer Darren Wilson shot Michael Brown dead in the streets of Ferguson. (I was in an airport that day, too, waiting for a flight to Cuba and watching Twitter explode with tweets from the scene of the murder. You texted me then and many times since, that you weren't so sure about coming to a country that could do this to its people, a country that went out of its way to destroy black life.) It's been a year of politicians stumbling to declare that all lives matter and reinstill the illusion of justice to the justice system. It's been a year in which police took more than three hundred black lives as protestors shut down bridges and highways across the country to remind the world that those lives matter.

I spent my twenties with a healthy distrust of the word *revolution*. When I was a kid, it was ancient American history or what *Star Wars* characters did—something heroic and distant. But I'm the son of a survivor of how wrong revolutions can go, the nephew of a revolutionary turned counterrevolutionary turned political prisoner. And these days, you're more likely to see *revolution* on a car ad than anywhere meaningful. Words mean things, we say again and again, but overuse and abuse can wear those meanings down, render them pale parodies of what they once were. And revolution, it seemed, had long since lost its meaning.

The Ferguson uprising changed that. The movement for black lives spread from city to city, spurned on by social media and the long-pent-up feeling that no social movement in recent memory has done anything but tiptoe toward justice. You can't tiptoe toward justice. You can't walk up to the door all polite and knock once or twice, hoping someone's home. Justice is a door that, when closed, must be kicked in. "No state," Baldwin wrote, "has been able to foresee or prevent the day when their most ruined and abject accomplice—or most expensively dressed prostitute—will growl, 'This far and no further.'" And maybe that day is more like a series of days, the whole year of protest that erupted between now and then, a culminating mass of days and nights, bodies laying down in intersections, symphony halls, strip malls, superhighways across this country, stopping traffic and business-as-usual, declaring by their very presence: "No further," and again, "No further."

I texted you updates as we marched: "Still safe and things are mostly calm. We've taken Columbus Circle. Helicopters overhead but cops can't seem to keep up with us or figure out where we're going next." They couldn't figure out where we were going next because we had no idea where we'd go next. We spun in an impossible, unruly snake through Midtown, spilled out into the streets and then the bridges and throughways. One night we shut down the Manhattan Bridge and pushed deep into Crown Heights, an army of flashing blue lights at our backs. With no coordination, no grant dictating our steps or signs, no leader, we marched in lockstep with hundreds of thousands of protestors across the United States and then the globe, and the simple, resonating demand that black lives matter laid bare the twin lies of American equality and exceptionalism. Even on the left, even in this age of exposed racial rifts, politicians still say with a straight face that this country was founded on principles of equality. Words mean things, we say again and again, but actions mean much more, and still as a nation, we worship the very slave owners who gave legal precedence to the notion of percentages of human beings. We scream *equality* and *freedom* while unabashedly modeling our actions on the fathers of genocide. The only way to rationalize this most American of contradictions is to devalue the lives of the slaughtered, as was done then, so it must be now, and so apologists remind us that those were the times, and they didn't know better, and on and on. But if those lives matter now then they mattered then, and the clapback stretches through history, unraveling all the creation myths this country has always held most sacred, toppling our many false idols and cleaning out our profaned temples.

There was a terrible hunger revealed in that ongoing funeral procession. So many showed up because so many must mourn, the trauma of bearing witness etched across the streets of America. And collective mourning became collective resistance, and the hunger born from so much witnessing and so little action over the years was the hunger to rebel. Revolution has sounded, as Tracy Chapman once sang, like a whisper. I heard it in my own writing on equality in publishing, demanding more than just reform, more than just diversity. Heard it in my friends and loved ones' quiet ferocity as we talked into the night. But suddenly it was a collective howl, it echoed through the streets and out across the world: "This far and no further."

It's that hunger that I was trying to understand back in college when I jotted that quote down. It felt like tracing along the clues of a murder mystery: something was wrong. I couldn't identify the crime, but I was aware of it, inside of me and in the whole world around me, and both were deeply connected. That's why Eqbal Ahmad's idea about primary contradiction tattooed itself on my brain. I knew from very early on that I was an artist, that art was my own form of medicine, both for myself and the world: a tool that could create or destroy. And I knew I profited from the crime—as a straight cis man, a Latino who isn't black, a citizen of this great disastrous nation. And I knew I suffered from this crime with no name, too, that it robbed everyone in its grasp of humanity and self, made us tools and killers and liars and suicides. There were so many myths to unravel, even just within my own heart, my own head, but mythology was something I could understand. There were myths that were lies and myths made from truth, and often the falsest ones were the most plausible and the truest filled with dragons and gods. Every journey is a crisis, a turning point, a shedding of myths, and mine began with the gnawing certainty that something did not add up. And in a way, this journey never ends, but in another sense, it ends where all great roads lead: to the discovery of voice.

This year, the desperate hunger born from so much mourning found its collective voice. It happened in the streets, but it also happened across the Internet, in journals, and late-night phone calls. The revolution wasn't televised—there we saw only burning cars and concerned pundits—but it was live-tweeted. And while my own revolution took place on the page and in the streets, yours was a much more personal one, profound and earthshaking in its own, very different, way. I watched you stand at the crossroads of despair, Nastassian. Watched fear wash over you, and uncertainty. As that ache detonated again and again, I know the temptation to shut down entirely loomed large. We arrived at Manley Airport in Kingston to return to New York, checked our bags and emptied our pockets into the plastic bins, took off shoes and belts and were patted down and X-rayed and then whisked up an escalator to the waiting area. Kingston was a distant smattering of lights across the bay and home seemed a long way off for both of us. Sandra Bland's face stared out from the television as broadcasters wondered through their phony cheer about her last moments on earth, languishing in that Texas jail cell. International travel is a closed circuit—once you're in flight, there's no turning back and then you're vomited directly into the hands of U.S. immigration officials, passport control, customs, sniffing dogs, and the forever fallout of 9/11. And even if you have nothing to hide, and we had nothing to hide, it feels like the cold machinery of the state closing around your neck. I thought about all the times I'd been "randomly" searched and quelled my own anxiety and turned to you, wondering if you would be freaking out, but you met me with a smile.

Tell them how their mother landed on hope amidst all the

despair, you told me weeks later when I said I didn't know how to write this essay. And in that I saw a miracle: your own journey, your own revolution, unraveling beside me and mine and also separate, a whole country and sea away. You chose hope, and the night is quiet and I write while you sleep—and this moment with all its weight and responsibility, this turning point in the world and our lives, is ours, and these words are for you.

—D

Message to My Daughters

EDWIDGE DANTICAT

Soon after the one-year anniversary of the fatal shooting of Michael Brown by the Ferguson police officer Darren Wilson, I was in Haiti, at the southernmost end of the country's border with the Dominican Republic, where hundreds of Haitian refugees had either been deported or driven out of the Dominican Republic by intimidation or threats. Many of these men and women had very little warning that they were going to be picked up or chased away and most of them had fled with nothing but the clothes on their backs.

It was a bright sunny day, but the air was thick with dust. As some friends and I walked through the makeshift resettlement camps on the Haitian side of the border, in a place called Pak Kado, it felt as though we, along with the residents of the camps, were floating through clouds. Around us were lean-tos made of cardboard boxes and sheets. Dust-covered children walked around looking dazed even while playing with pebbles that stood in for marbles, or while flying plastic bags as kites. Elderly people stood on the edge of food and clothes distribution lines, some too weak to wade into the crowd. Later the elderly, along with pregnant women and the disabled, would be given special consideration by the priest and nuns who were giving out the only food available to the camp dwellers, but the food would always run out before they could get to everyone.

A few days after leaving Haiti and returning to the United States, I read a Michael Brown anniversary opinion piece in *The Washington Post* written by Raha Jorjani, an immigration attorney and law professor. In her essay, Jorjani argues that African Americans living in the United States could easily qualify as refugees. Citing many recent cases of police brutality and killings of unarmed black men, women, and children, she wrote:

> Suppose a client walked into my office and told me that police officers in his country had choked a man to death over a petty crime. Suppose he said police fatally shot another man in the back as he ran away. That they arrested a woman during a traffic stop and placed her in jail, where she died three days later. That a 12-year-old boy in his country was shot and killed by the police as he played in the park.
>
> Suppose he told me that all of those victims were from the same ethnic community—a community whose members fear being harmed, tortured or killed by police or prison guards. And that this is true in cities and towns across his nation. At that point, as an immigration lawyer, I'd tell him he had a strong claim for asylum protection under U.S. law.

This is not the first time that the idea of African Americans as internal or external refugees has been floated or applied. The six-million-plus African Americans who

MESSAGE TO MY DAUGHTERS

migrated from the rural south to urban centers in the northern United States for more than half a century during the Great Migration were often referred to as refugees, as were those people internally displaced by Hurricane Katrina.

Having now visited many refugee and displacement camps, the label "refugee" at first seemed an extreme designation to assign to citizens of one of the richest countries in the world, especially if it is assigned on a singular basis to those who are black. Still, compared to the relative wealth of the rest of the society, a particularly run-down Brooklyn public housing project where a childhood friend used to live had all the earmarks of a refugee camp. It occupied one of the least desirable parts of town and provided only the most basic necessities. A nearby dilapidated school, where I attended junior high, could have easily been on the edge of that refugee settlement, where the primary daily task was to keep the children occupied, rather than engaged and learning. Aside from a few overly devoted teachers, we were often on our own. We, immigrant blacks and African Americans alike, were treated by those who housed us, and were in charge of schooling us, as though we were members of a group in transit. The message we always heard from those who were meant to protect us: that we should either die or go somewhere else. This is the experience of a refugee.

I have seen state abuses up close, both in Haiti, where I was born under a ruthless dictatorship, and in New York, where I migrated to a working-class and predominantly African, African American, and Caribbean neighborhood in Brooklyn at the age of twelve. In the Haiti of the 1970s and early '80s, the violence was overtly political. Government detractors were dragged out of their homes, imprisoned, beaten, or killed. Sometimes their bodies were left out in the streets, in the hot sun, for extended periods, to intimidate neighbors.

In New York, the violence seemed a bit more subtle, though no less pervasive. When I started riding the city bus to high school, I observed that a muffled radio message from an annoyed bus driver—about someone talking too loud or not having the right fare—was all it took to make the police rush in, drag a young man off the bus, and beat him into submission on the sidewalk. There were no cell phone cameras back then to record such abuse, and most of us were too terrified to demand a badge number.

Besides, many of us had fled our countries as exiles, migrants, and refugees just to escape this kind of military or police aggression; we knew how deadly a confrontation with an armed and uniformed authoritarian figure could be. Still, every now and then a fellow traveler would summon his or her courage and, dodging the swaying baton, or screaming from a distance, would yell some variation of "Stop it! This is a child! A child!"

Of course, not all of the police's victims were children. Abner Louima, a family friend, was thirty years old when he was mistaken for someone who had punched a police officer outside a Brooklyn nightclub, on August 9, 1997, sixteen years to the day before Michael Brown was killed. Abner was arrested, beaten with fists, as well as with police radios, flashlights, and nightsticks, and then sexually assaulted with the wooden handle of a toilet plunger or a broom inside a precinct bathroom. After Abner, there was Amadou Diallo, a Guinean immigrant, who was hit by nineteen of the forty-one bullets aimed at him as he retrieved his wallet from his pocket. Then there was Patrick Dorismond, the U.S.-born child of Haitian immigrants, who died trying to convince undercover cops that he was not a drug dealer.

These are only a few among the cases from my era that made the news. There was also sixty-six-year-old Eleanor Bumpurs, who, thirteen years before Abner's assault, was killed by police with a twelve-gauge shotgun inside her own apartment. I have no doubt there were many others. We marched for all of them in the Louima/Diallo/Dorismond decade. We carried signs and chanted "No Justice! No Peace!" and "Whose Streets? Our Streets!" even while fearing the latter would never be true. The streets belonged to the people with the uniforms and the guns. The streets were never ours. Our sons and brothers, fathers and uncles, our mothers and sisters, daughters and nieces, our neighbors were, and still are, prey.

My father, a Brooklyn cab driver, used to half joke that police did not beat him up because, at sixty-five years old, he was too skinny and too old, and not worth the effort. Every now and then, when he was randomly stopped by a police officer and deigned to ask why, rather than a beating, he would be given a handful of unwarranted traffic citations that would wipe out a few weeks' hard-earned wages. Today, one might generously refer to such acts as micro-aggressions. That is, until they turn major and deadly, until other unarmed black bodies, with nowhere to go for refuge, find themselves in the path of yet another police officer's or armed vigilante's gun.

When it was announced that Darren Wilson would not be indicted for the killing of Michael Brown, I kept thinking of Abner Louima, whose assault took place when Michael Brown was just eighteen months old. Abner and I have known each other for years. Both our families have attended the same Creole-speaking church for decades, so I called him to hear his thoughts about Michael Brown's killer going free. If anyone could understand all those broken hearts, all the rage, all the desperation, the yearning for justice, what it is to be a member of a seemingly marooned and persecuted group, I thought, he would.

Abner Louima, unlike Michael Brown, had survived. He went on with his life, moved from New York City to south Florida, started businesses. He has a daughter and two sons. One son was eighteen years old when we spoke, the same age Michael Brown was when he died.

How does he feel, I asked him, each time he hears that yet another black person was killed or nearly killed by police?

"It reminds me that our lives mean nothing," he replied.

We are in America because our lives meant nothing to those in power in the countries where we came from. Yet we come here to realize that our lives also mean nothing here. Some of us try to distance ourselves from this reality, thinking that because we are another type of "other" — immigrants, migrants, refugees—this is not our problem, nor one we can solve. But ultimately we realize the precarious nature of citizenship here: that we too are prey, and that those who have been in this country for generations—walking, living, loving in the same skin we're in—they too can suddenly become refugees.

Parents are often too nervous to broach difficult subjects with their children. Love. Sex. Death. Race. But some parents are forced to have these conversations early. Too early. A broken heart might lead to questions we'd rather not answer, as might an inappropriate gesture, the death of a loved one, or the murder of a stranger.

Each time a black person is killed in a manner that's clearly racially motivated, either by a police officer or a vigilante civilian, I ask myself if the time has come for me to talk to my daughters about Abner Louima and the long list of dead that have come since. My daughters have met Abner, but I have never told them about his past, even though his past is a future they might have to face.

Why don't I tell them? My decision is about more than avoiding a difficult conversation. The truth is, I do not want my daughters to grow up as I did, terrified of the country and the world they live in. But is it irresponsible of me to not alert them to the potentially life-altering, or even life-ending horrors they might face as young black women?

The night President Barack Obama was first elected (would he too qualify for refugee status?), my oldest daughter was three and I was in the last weeks of my pregnancy with my second. When President Obama was inaugurated for the first time, I was cradling both my little girls in my arms.

To think, I remember telling my husband, our daughters will never know a world in which the president of their country has not been black. Indeed, as we watched President Obama's inaugural speech, my oldest daughter was shocked that no woman had ever been president of the United States. That day, the world ahead for my girls seemed full of greater possibility—if not endless possibilities, then at least greater than those for generations past. Many more doors suddenly seemed open to my girls, and the "joyous daybreak" evoked by Martin Luther King, Jr., in his "I Have a Dream" speech, a kind of jubilee, seemed to have emerged. However, it quickly became clear that this one man was not going to take all of us with him into the postracial promised land. Or that he even had full access to it. Constant talk of "wanting him to fail" was racially tinged, as were the "birther" investigations, and the bigoted commentaries and jokes by both elected officials and ordinary folk. One of the most consistent attacks against the president, was that, like my husband and myself, he was born elsewhere and was not *really* American.

Like Barack Obama's father, many of us had brought our black bodies to America from somewhere else. Some of us, like the president, were the children of such people. We are people who need to have two different talks with our black offspring: one about why we're here and the other about why it's not always a promised land for people who look like us.

In his own version of "The Talk," James Baldwin wrote to his nephew James in "My Dungeon Shook," "You were born in a society which spelled out with brutal clarity, and in as many ways as possible that you were a worthless human being."

That same letter could have been written to a long roster of dead young men and women, whose dungeons shook, but whose chains did not completely fall off. Among these very young people are Oscar Grant, Aiyana Stanley-Jones, Rekia Boyd, Kimani Gray, Renisha McBride, Trayvon Martin, Michael Bell, Tamir Rice, Michael Brown, Sandra Bland, and counting. It's sad to imagine what these young people's letters from their loved ones may have said. Had their favorite uncle notified them that they could qualify for refugee status within their own country? Did their mother or father, grandmother or grandfather warn them to not walk in white neighborhoods, to, impossibly, avoid police officers, to never play in a public park, to stay away from neighborhood watchmen, to never go to a neighbor's house, even if to seek help from danger?

I am still, in my own mind, drafting a "My Dungeon Shook" letter to my daughters. It often begins like this. *Dear Mira and Leila, I've put off writing this letter to you for as long as I can, but I don't think I can put it off any longer. Please know that there will be times when some people might be hostile or even violent to you for reasons that have nothing to do with your beauty, your humor, or your grace, but only your race and the color of your skin. Please don't let this restrict your freedom, break your spirit, or kill your joy. And if possible do everything you can to change the world so that your generation of brown and black men, women, and children will be the last who experience all this. And please do live your best lives and achieve your full potential. Love deeply. Be joyful. In Jubilee, Mom.*

To my draft of this letter, I often add snippets of Baldwin.

"I tell you this because I love you and please don't you ever forget it," Baldwin reminded his James. "Know whence you came. If you know whence you came, there is no limit to where you can go."

"The world is before you," I want to tell my daughters, "and you need not take it or leave it as it was when you came in."

I want to look happily forward. I want to be optimistic. I want to have a dream. I want to live in jubilee. I want my daughters to feel that they have the power to at least try to change things, even in a world that resists change with more strength than they have. I want to tell them they can overcome everything, if they are courageous, resilient, and brave. Paradoxically, I also want to tell them their crowns have already been bought and paid for and that all they have to do is put them on their heads. But the world keeps tripping me up. My certainty keeps flailing.

So I took them to the border, the one between Haiti and the Dominican Republic, where hundreds of refugees were living, or rather existing. There they saw and helped comfort men, women, and children who look like them, but are stateless, babies with not even a bedsheet between them and a dirt floor, young people who may not be killed by bullets but by the much slower assault of disease.

"These are all our causes," I tried to both tell and show

them, brown and black bodies living with "certain uncertainty," to use Frantz Fanon's words, black bodies fleeing oppression, persecution, and poverty, wherever they are.

"You think your pain and your heartbreak are unprecedented in the history of the world, but then you read," James Baldwin wrote. Or you see. Or you weep. Or you pray. Or you speak. Or you write. Or you fight so that one day everyone will be able to walk the earth as though they, to use Baldwin's words, have "a right to be here." May that day come, Mira and Leila, when you can finally claim those crowns of yours and put them on your heads. When that day of jubilee finally arrives, all of us will be there with you, walking, heads held high, crowns a-glitter, because we do have a right to be here.

Acknowledgments

I'd like to thank all of the writers who contributed to this book. I wasn't asking an easy thing of them when I solicited their creative work; instead, I was asking them to write toward the hurt, to wrestle with the ugly truths that plague us in this country. Each of the writers did just that, and they did so beautifully. My editor, Kathryn Belden, believed in this book before I could even articulate why I wanted to work on it. She edited this collection tirelessly. She makes me a better writer, and I am so grateful to work with her. Her assistant, David Lamb, ushered the book through the first round of edits, communicated with the contributors about contracts, and aided in copyedits. I'm thankful for Jennifer Lyons, my agent, who has always been my advocate. I am indebted to Scribner, who welcomed this book into their catalog and me into their coterie of writers. Finally, I'd like to remember the sage, fierce artist who inspired this book, James Baldwin. I hope our work makes you proud.

Contributors

CAROL ANDERSON is the Samuel Candler Dobbs Professor and chair of African American Studies at Emory University and the author of *White Rage: The Unspoken Truth of Our Racial Divide* and *Eyes Off the Prize: The United Nations and the African American Struggle for Human Rights, 1944–1955*, which was awarded the Myrna F. Bernath Book Award and the Gustavus Myers Outstanding Book Award and was selected as a finalist for the Truman Book Award and the W. E. B. Du Bois Book Award.

JERICHO BROWN has published two poetry collections, *Please* and *The New Testament*, and has been the recipient of the Whiting Writers' Award, the American Book Award, a fellowship at the Radcliffe Institute for Advanced Study, and a National Endowment for the Arts grant. He is an associate professor of English and creative writing at Emory University in Atlanta.

GARNETTE CADOGAN is editor-at-large of *Nonstop Metropolis: A New York City Atlas* (coedited by Rebecca Solnit and Joshua Jelly-Schapiro). He is currently a visiting fellow at the Institute for Advanced Studies in Culture at the

University of Virginia, and a visiting scholar at the Institute for Public Knowledge at New York University. He writes about culture and the arts for various publications, and is at work on a book about walking.

EDWIDGE DANTICAT, born in Haiti and raised in New York, has written both fiction and nonfiction for adults and children. Her memoir, *Brother, I'm Dying*, was awarded the National Book Critics Circle Award, and was finalist for the National Book Award, as was her short story collection *Krik? Krak!* She is a 2009 MacArthur Fellow.

RACHEL KAADZI GHANSAH is an essayist and critic whose writing has appeared in the *Believer*, *Rolling Stone*, the *Paris Review*, *Transition*, and elsewhere. She was a finalist for the National Magazine Award, and she is a contributing writer for the *New York Times Magazine*. Her first book, *The Explainers and Explorers*, examines twenty-first-century America within the context of what it means to be black, brave, and self-defined, and it will be published by Scribner in 2017.

MITCHELL S. JACKSON is the author of *The Residue Years*, which won the Ernest J. Gaines Award and was a finalist for the Center for Fiction's Flaherty-Dunnan First Novel Prize, the PEN/Hemingway Award for Debut Fiction, and the Hurston/Wright Legacy Award. He is a recipient of a Whiting Award and teaches writing at NYU, where he earned an MFA in creative writing.

HONORÉE FANONNE JEFFERS is a poet, fiction writer, and critic. She is the author of four books of poetry and is at work on her first novel. Her fifth poetry book, in progress, *The Age of Phillis*, imagines the life and times of the eighteenth-century poet Phillis Wheatley, the first (known) black woman to publish a book. The recipient of fellowships from the National Endowment for the Arts and the Witter Bynner Foundation through the Library of Congress, Jeffers is an elected member of the American Antiquarian Society, an organization to which fourteen U.S. presidents have been elected. She teaches at the University of Oklahoma.

KIMA JONES's work has appeared in *Guernica*, *NPR*, *PANK*, *Scratch Magazine*, and *The Rumpus*, and she has received fellowships from PEN Center USA, Yaddo, and the MacDowell Colony.

KIESE LAYMON is associate professor of English and Africana Studies at Vassar College and a recent Grisham Writer in Residence at the University of Mississippi. He is the author of the novel *Long Division*, which was selected as a best book of 2013 by *Buzzfeed*, *The Believer*, *Salon*, *Guernica*, *Library Journal*, and the *Chicago Tribune*, and an essay collection, *How to Slowly Kill Yourself and Others in America*. He is a columnist at *The Guardian*, and his forthcoming memoir, *Heavy*, will be published by Scribner.

DANIEL JOSÉ OLDER is the author of the Bone Street Rumba urban fantasy series (Roc Books, 2015 and 2016) and the

Young Adult novel *Shadowshaper* (Scholastic, 2015), which was shortlisted for the Kirkus Prize in Young Readers' Literature. He coedited the Locus and World Fantasy Award–nominated anthology *Long Hidden: Speculative Fiction from the Margins of History*. You can find Daniel's thoughts on writing, read dispatches from his decadelong career as an NYC paramedic, and hear his music at danieljoseolder.net and @djolder on Twitter.

EMILY RABOTEAU is the author of *The Professor's Daughter: A Novel* and *Searching for Zion: The Quest for Home in the African Diaspora*, winner of the 2014 American Book Award and finalist for the Hurston Wright Legacy Award. Her distinctions include a Pushcart Prize, a literature fellowship from the National Endowment for the Arts, and the Chicago Tribune's Nelson Algren Award. She is a professor of English at the City College of New York, in Harlem, where she codirects the MFA program in creative writing. Her next novel is in the works.

CLAUDIA RANKINE is the author of five collections of poetry including *Citizen: An American Lyric*, which won the National Book Critics Circle Award for Poetry in 2015, the PEN/Open Book Award, the PEN Literary Award, and the NAACP Image Award, and was a finalist for the National Book Award. She lives in California, where she is the Aerol Arnold Professor of English at the University of Southern California.

CONTRIBUTORS

CLINT SMITH is a National Science Foundation Graduate Research Fellow and a doctoral candidate in education at Harvard University. He was a 2014 National Poetry Slam champion and has two popular TED Talks, *The Danger of Silence* and *How to Raise a Black Son in America*. His poems and essays have appeared in *The New Yorker*, *The Guardian*, and *The American Literary Review*. He is the author of the poetry collection *Counting Descent*.

NATASHA TRETHEWEY is the author of four poetry collections, *Domestic Work*, *Bellocq's Ophelia*; *Native Guard* (which won the 2007 Pulitzer Prize) and *Thrall*, as well as a book of nonfiction, *Beyond Katrina: A Meditation on the Mississippi Gulf Coast*. Her column, "Poem," appears weekly in the *New York Times Magazine*. She teaches at Emory University as the Robert W. Woodruff Professor of English and creative writing and has served for two terms as the United States Poet Laureate (2012–14).

WENDY S. WALTERS is the author of *Multiply/Divide: On the American Real and Surreal*; *Troy, Michigan*; *Longer I Wait, More You Love Me*; and a chapbook, *Birds of Los Angeles*. She is associate professor of creative writing and literature at The New School.

ISABEL WILKERSON is the first African American woman to win a Pulitzer Prize in journalism, awarded for her coverage of the 1993 Midwestern floods and for her profile of a ten-year-old boy caring for his four siblings. She is the author of the *New York Times* bestseller *The Warmth of Other Suns*, which won the National Book Critics Circle Award for Nonfiction in 2010.

KEVIN YOUNG has edited five collections of poetry and published eight poetry collections of his own, including *For the Confederate Dead, Book of Hours*, and *Jelly Roll*, which was a finalist for the National Book Award for Poetry, as well as *Blue Laws: Selected and Uncollected Poems, 1995–2015*. He is also the author of *The Grey Album: On the Blackness of Blackness*, an encyclopedic nonfiction book examining through Jay Z's *The Black Album* and The Beatles's *The White Album* how African American culture *is* in many ways American culture, which won the Pen/Open Book Award and the Graywolf Press Nonfiction Prize and was a finalist for the National Book Critics Circle Award for Criticism.

Permissions

ABOUT THE EDITOR

Jesmyn Ward received her MFA from the University of Michigan and is currently an associate professor of creative writing at Tulane University. She is the author of the novels *Where the Line Bleeds* and *Salvage the Bones*, which won the 2011 National Book Award and was a finalist for the New York Public Library Young Lions Fiction Award and the Dayton Literary Peace Prize. She is also the author of the memoir *Men We Reaped*, which was a finalist for the National Book Critics Circle Award and the Hurston/Wright Legacy Award and won the Chicago Tribune Heartland Prize and the Media for a Just Society Award.